THE BOOK OF
SYMBOLS

THE BOOK OF SYMBOLS

JANA GARAI

LORRIMER PUBLISHING   LONDON

© Jana Garai 1973

First published in Great Britain in 1973
by Lorrimer Publishing Limited,
47 Dean Street, London W1

ISBN 0-85647-024-4

ACKNOWLEDGMENTS

Cover and titles designed by
Peter Warne & Associates
Acknowledgments and thanks are due to
Hulton Educational Publications Limited
for permission to reproduce six illustrations
from their publications
Town Ecology and *Woodland Ecology*

Manufactured in Great Britain by
Villiers Publications Ltd. London NW5.

CONTENTS

To Dr. Louis A. Nichols

INTRODUCTION

Ex Umbris et Imaginibus in Veritatem!
(From shadows and symbols into the truth.)
John Henry, Cardinal Newman, 1801-1890
Epitaph at Edgbaston, composed by himself.

SYMBOLISM has been defined as an art of thinking in images; an art said to have been gradually lost to the western world through the disastrous theories of Descartes and others, some three hundred years ago. Even though it may be a forgotten language, the study of religions, psychology and the arts reveals that its loss is only on the conscious level, and that symbol and myth making is still a natural condition and activity of the unconscious mind. The first interpretations of the strange world of the unconscious from which these symbols arise, were made by Freud. Jung went beyond Freud and restored a spiritual significance to these images, emphasizing man's quest for God. The instinctive attitudes of man which Freud described as 'primitive fantasies', became the archetypal images of Jung. These inherent images and emotions are universal symbols expressing psychic growth and evolution towards the god-like nature of man.

A symbol is an outwardly projected image of the inward feelings and thoughts of man. Because certain concepts such as resurrection or death are beyond human understanding, they can only be conveyed by the use of symbolism. A symbol suggests what it conceals and cannot easily be explained because it is based on analogy; it is a visible sign of the invisible.

Although the words symbol and sign are often used interchangeably there is a distinction between the two. A sign is intentionally used to represent a definite object or an idea. It may be a badge or an emblem but it denotes and defines and is made by man. A symbol has much deeper meaning than a sign and refers to something mysterious and unknown which has been created by the part of man that is god.

Many philosophers have claimed that analogy is primitive and irrational and yet it is the basis of all symbolic theory. It is a means by which man has best expressed his inner conflicts and realities and has come to know them. Despite our scientific age of rationalism the imagery of our ancestral fears, hopes and desires survives still in a repressed and impoverished form through mythology and rites of archaic, primitive or eastern cultures. Through analogy symbolism relates the outer world to the inner, the spiritual to the material. The process of creation and the cycle of life, for example, were explained by ancient Egyptians through the myth of Osiris who was killed by his brother and resurrected by Isis. In Greece, Dionysus was slaughtered by the Titans, and Plutarch describes him as 'the god who is destroyed, who disappears, who relinquishes life and then is born again.' Another symbolic analogy is that of the bridge and the rainbow. The two are synonymous in symbolism and represent the link between man and god or between that which is perceived and the unseen. A rainbow marked the end of the flood and was a symbol of God's covenant to the Israelites that such a deluge would never again 'destroy all flesh'.

We are the heirs of Greece and Rome, of Judaism and Christianity, though much insight can also be gained from other cultures. Through images of distant civilizations, shadows of the Homeric man and symbols of early prophets, we reach for the universal truth.

EARTH & HER GIFTS

THAT EARTH gives birth to man is a universal belief pervading every religion, culture and mythology. As a Mother Goddess, she not only produces food and shelter for man, but represents his origin and creation. As a divinity, earth has existed since palaeolithic times and has remained the primary symbol of life.

This image of the earth as woman or mother who gives birth to all things is well illustrated in the mythologies of the American Indians. These reveal that the first men lived for a certain time in the bowels of earth itself. There was always darkness within the womb, but one day, a man found an opening and climbed out to discover the light and beauty of the surface. Soon others joined him and remained in the sun, hunting deer and feasting on the vegetation. As an allegory of the period of gestation and birth itself, the legend is obvious; but if this is how the Indian regarded the earth, it is not surprising that he often refused to till the land. For him, farming would have represented the wounding of his own mother, as the soil was her flesh, the stones her bones, and grass and corn, the hair of her head.

Even the more highly evolved Greek myth refers to Mother Earth as first emerging from all chaos. According to the Olympian legend of creation, earth gave birth to Uranus while she slept. And he, in gratitude, poured rain into her secret clefts, forming rivers and seas, and she bore flowers and grass and trees, together with birds and beasts. This mystical identification of woman with the land is further borne out by the Koran which says: ' Your women are unto you as fields ', while the man is looked upon as the bestower of the seed.

Even in our present European culture there exists an underlying feeling of mystical union with the native earth. This is not only a sentimental love of country and homeland, but a more universal, even religious concept of: ' Earth to earth, ashes to ashes, dust to dust; in sure and certain hopes of the Resurrection unto eternal life '. This mystic bond of man to earth lies deeper than his attachment to his family and own kind. Perhaps his unconscious belief that he came from the earth gave rise to certain notions that children were born of rivers or caves, or that they were brought by frogs and storks. Strangely enough, the Romans used to call bastards ' the sons of the earth ', just as some langauges today call them ' children of flowers ' or ' natural children '.

If we conceive of the earth as the universal creator and nurse, then a woman bearing a child does no more than complete the function. At death the desire to return to the Earth Mother or to the native soil is so profound that it is deeply rooted not only in legend, but in our present sense of tradition.

Since ancient times, the northern hemisphere has represented light, corresponding to the Chinese principle of Yang or the positive. But the southern hemisphere has been linked with darkness or the negative Yin, and in history, cultural movements have most often passed from north to south. As a whole, the Earth Mother is the guardian of justice and morality, and from the days of ancient Greece when bloodshed and incest made her barren, so does evil and crime offend her still.

AIR

'Ah yet would God this flesh of mine might be
Where air might wash and long leaves cover me '.
Laus Veneris
Algernon Charles Swinburne

AIR IS A VAST, unknown space which surrounds man and his earth; a subtle matter giving warmth and cold, water and drought, and a void from which the original vibrations emerged. Among the many different theories disputing the prime cause of the creation of the universe, air has probably received the greatest place of honour. Like the element of fire, it is related to the male quality of action and although it feeds the flame with oxygen it does also, through compression, produce an igniting spark. The foundations of alchemy were based on the transmutation of the four elements, but as each one of these elements grew, as it were, through the changes occurring in the other, they all still needed the final, animating breath of the creator. Air is a form of that creative ' breath ' which God expelled into the nostrils of Adam to bring him to life and which He exhaled with every word commanding the Creation.

Another and a more violent aspect of air is shown in the winds which, in many mythologies, were personified as hostile or benevolent gods. In a Teutonic legend of the Creation, the frozen giant Ymir was blown upon by the warm south wind and as he began to melt in his cold surroundings, the first man and woman emerged from his sweat. In Egypt and Greece, the wind had certain powers of evil and was identified with the wicked god Set, or Typhon, who was the spirit of the hurricane and a father of many monsters. But for the Greeks this menacing image was reversed from the moment that the great north wind, Boreas who lived in the mountains of Thrace, dispersed the invading fleet of Xerxes. The same god-wind Boreas, at a time when matriarchy dominated mythology and religion, was credited with powers of regeneration and women conceived as mares bred their foals, by turning their hindquarters to the air.

12

FIRE

' Some say the world will end in fire,
Some say in ice.
From what I've tasted of desire
I hold with those who favour fire '.

Fire and Ice
Robert Frost

AS ONE OF THE four elements, fire is a symbol of life and death or good and evil. Most primitive races saw it as the sun on earth and personified it as a monster breathing flames from its jaws. At other times it was a salamander which, according to tradition, can live within fire without being harmed. Punishment and purification by fire was early recognised in the Bible, and God's judgment against the evils of Babylon was that ' her high gates shall be burned with fire; and the people shall labour in vain, and the folk in the fire, and they shall be weary '. As the Gospel according to St Matthew condemned bad Christians to the fate of a barren fruit tree which must be ' cast into the fire ', so did the flames in early paintings of the apostles mean torments of hell for the heathen.

To the Egyptians a fire was symbolic of control and the superiority of spiritual development and energy. The Greeks associated it with deity in their worship of Prometheus, who brought it to men by stealth from the gods. To the Israelites, God showed His constant presence with a shining pillar of fire, during their wanderings in the desert at night. The Mithraic cult which had been in existence some five hundred years before Christ, also held the sun and its fire as the chief source of goodness, conquering evil and darkness. Anthropologists believe that many rites of the primitives, including the carrying of torches and the lighting of bonfires to stimulate the growth of crops and the well-being of the people, correspond to our Christmas lights, fireworks and other festivals of fire.

Paracelsus, a sixteenth-century alchemist and doctor, pointed out a parallel between fire and life, in that both must feed upon other lives in order to keep alive.

WATER

' And watching, with eternal lids apart,
Like nature's patient, sleepless Eremite,
The moving waters at their priestlike task
Of pure ablution round earth's human shores '.
Bright Star, Sonnet
John Keats

' WATER NEVER rests, neither by day nor by night. When flowing above, it causes rain and dew. When flowing below, it forms streams and rivers. Water is outstanding in doing good '. This is the way in which Lao-Tse describes the cycle of water in nature as the essence of life. But in nearly all myths and legends of the Creation, water is also symbolic of the actual source of life itself, for it was from the great abyss filled with water that life first emerged. As a natural resource it is mentioned in the Scriptures more often than any other, and because it was of such great importance, it became very early a sacred element in ritual and worship. In the East water is regarded as the preserver of life, circulating through nature also in the form of fluids such as blood, rain and sap; it is a maternal element in the sense that it gave birth to all.

The purifying qualities of water were already recognised in Babylon and Assyria, where the great Euphrates was the principal river used for cleansing and purging rituals. The act of immersion in water, which later became the sacrament of baptism, signifies the washing away of sin or impurity. It is symbolic of the annihilation of evil and the consequent regeneration of man or the spirit. In a much broader sense, the great floods throughout ancient history held the same symbolic meaning.

All stretches of water, rivers and springs were deified in early times and most shrines tended to be placed near them. Water divinities were numerous and hydromancy was practised widely by the Egyptian priests and sorcerers. This divination by water was probably the origin of our modern 'tea-leaf' readings. Important factors in these auguries were the colour of the water, its ebb and flow and the patterns it produced when pebbles were dropped into pools. Another accomplished art that the Egyptians claimed to possess was the power to divide water so that it could stand aside, exposing the beds of rivers or seas. Thus, according to *Exodus*, Moses stretched out his hand and parted the Red Sea, allowing the children of Israel to pass by as if on dry land. The art of dowsing is still being used to discover the exact location of underground water, and the forked stick of hazel known to the Romans as 'virgula furcate' was reintroduced to England in the reign of Elizabeth I.

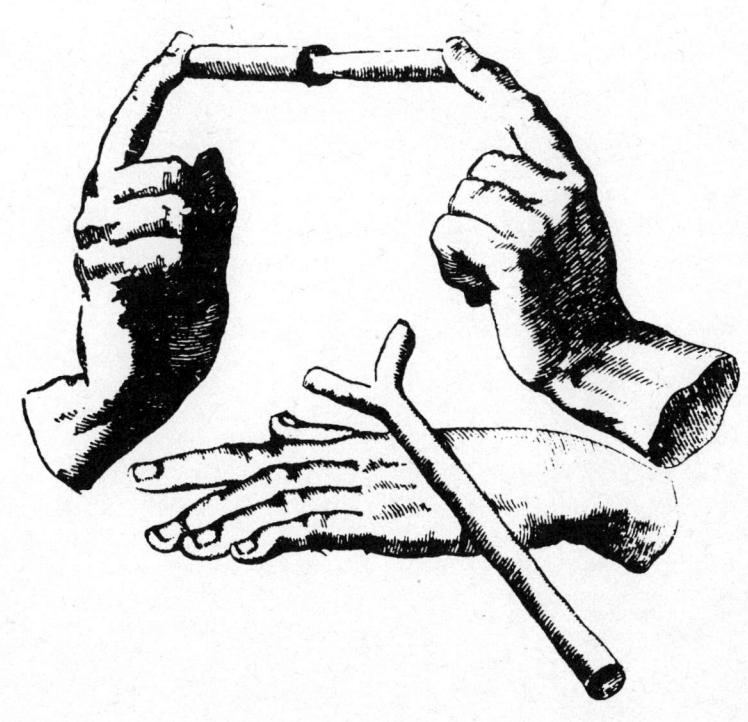

15

STONE

'Awake! for Morning in the Bowl of Night
Has flung the Stone that puts the Stars to flight'.
The Rubaiyat of Omar Khayyam
Edward Fitzgerald

THE SOLIDITY and hardness of a stone always conveyed to man the idea of strength and unity. In a world constantly subjected to death, decay and biological change, it was an impressive object of durability and worship. In the process of volcanic eruptions, stones served to explain the origin of life, as did the meteors which literally fell from heaven. Early civilizations set up these stones with great veneration and made them the primal object of religious rites. One of the most famous of such stones, a meteorite, was worshipped as a symbol of the sun in Emessa, Syria. Another, the Black Stone of the Kaab in Mecca, is still kissed by every pilgrim to the Great Mosque. This is also a meteorite and although it was deified centuries before Mohammed, it is now an object of sanctity to all Moslems, who believe that it was white when it fell from heaven but turned black because of the sins of mankind.

Fable and legend refer to many magical stones. The Aetites, or eagle stones, found in the nests of these birds, reputedly healed 'falling sickness' and prevented untimely birth. According to Pliny, 'the stone in question is big with another inside it, which rattles, as if in a jar when you shake it'. The analogy of this description is, of course, to a foetus contained within a womb. The touchstone, which was usually a dark piece of basinite or jasper, was the famed lapis lydius of the Romans. It was used to test matter for its gold content and as Thomas Fuller, in the seventeenth century, remarked: 'Men have a touchstone whereby to try gold; but gold is the touchstone whereby to try men'.

SILVER

'Just for a handful of silver he left us,
Just for a riband to stick in his coat'.
The Lost Leader
Robert Browning

A PRECIOUS metal tested by fire and white in colour, silver is a symbol of purity and chastity. 'Silver-tongued' was a name given to the evangelists and many later preachers such as Henry Smith in sixteenth-century England. It referred to their magnificent eloquence and probably took its origin from the Twelfth Psalm, which reads: 'The words of the Lord are pure words: as silver tried in a furnace of earth, purified seven times'.

Silver is a moon metal associated with the occult, darkness and the unconscious, and as such, it is in opposition to the gold of the sun which is symbolic of light and of life. In the Tarot, however, the whole concept of unity between the two is very beautifully expressed. The fourteenth card, called Temperance or the Angel of Time, shows a figure pouring liquid from a silver to a golden cup. If the silver represents the moon, and the gold the sun, while the flowing liquid is a spiritual force, then the conscious and the unconscious are combined into a greater knowledge, power and strength.

The purity of silver and its connection with the moon made it the perfect metal for the making of talismans and amulets, and Mohammed himself forbade the use of any other substance. An eighteenth-century book of magic says that a talisman engraved on silver when the moon is well aspected, will make one cheerful, healthy, honoured and rich; but a talisman of lead buried near a home will bring evil to the household.

GOLD

' Whereas gold is the kindest of all hosts
when it shines in the sky, it comes an evil
guest unto those that receive it in their hand '.
The Malignity of Herodotus
Plutarch

GOLD, BECAUSE it is a valuable metal and the colour of sunlight, corresponds to the mystic aspect of the sun. It is symbolic of all that is superior and divine in the same sense that the sun refers to the source of all purity, holiness and goodness. Anything golden or made of gold possesses a quality of perfection, but as an object of worldly wealth, it is often condemned in the Bible and by legend. In the story of King Midas who turned all he touched to gold, or of Aaron who worshipped the golden calf, it is a symbol of greed and idolatory; but it can also be the essential element of spiritual riches as in the myths of the quest for hidden treasure.

The symbolism of gold as the perfect metal is best explained in terms of alchemy and its connection with the spiritual world. The funda-mental maxim of a true alchemist was: ' Who-ever wanted to make gold must begin with gold because a man cannot find truth unless he is true himself, or God unless he has God within him '. The main stages of the ' Great Work ', also symbolic of the spiritual evolu-tion of man, intended to copy the cycle of nature which moves from birth to decay, death and rebirth. A base metal had to be reduced to the so-called ' first matter ', which changed the form of the metal, but at the same time released the hidden essence of life within it. This process was similar to that of a soul being released from a body by death. When that essence was further combined with other sub-stances and underwent more complex trans-mutation, it was eventually capable of produc-ing the perfect metal. This was the Philosopher's Stone, or the state of completion which in turn had the supreme power of turning all things into gold.

The fabled elixir of life was also related to gold. Paracelsus, the greatest occulist of the sixteenth century, claimed to have made it from gold. In its liquid form it was the perfect medication and particularly good for disorders of the heart, because gold and the heart are ruled by the sun. A recipe exists which gives the secret of making 'potable gold'. The ingredients are three pints of red wine vinegar, the ashes of a block of tin, one ounce of gold and a little salt.

The connection between gold and the sanctity of kings is a very ancient one and its roots again lie in the symbolism of gold as a state of glory. One example of this in English history was the belief that scrofula, a disease of the lymphatic glands, could only be cured by a king's touch. 'Healing gold' was the name given to the coins distributed during the ceremonial touchings first introduced by Henry VII. This custom ended, however, in 1712 when it was last practised on Dr Johnson by Queen Anne, apparently without any effect.

GEM

' How many a thing which we cast to the ground,
When others pick it up becomes a gem '.
Modern Love
George Meredith

THE GEM AND the jewel are symbolic of superior knowledge and spiritual truth. The theme of the quest belongs to all mythologies and hidden treasures guarded by dragons or monsters allude to man's struggle to conquer all in order to gain this knowledge. Jung believes that many folk tales concerning gems hidden in caves and buried in the ground, actually refer to the intuitive and unconscious knowledge that we all possess.

For the ancients, many precious stones possessed magical and curative powers. Each sign of the Zodiac, for instance, carries its particular stone. The Greeks believed that there existed a stone which cured snake bites and that this had to be ground to powder and sprinkled on the wound. A jasper worn by ploughmen ensured fertility of their land; and for the Chinese, jade was the purest and the most divine precious stone of all, and its powers were endless. Curiously enough, it was believed that all darker stones were male and those of a lighter shade had feminine traits. Browning, for example, speaks of Saul's bejewelled turban with ' all its lordly male-sapphires, and rubies courageous at heart '.

In Biblical times, there was a custom of building jewels and precious metals into palaces and temples; the *Book of Revelation* mentions the names of the twelve apostles engraved on gems and placed into the foundations of a city wall. Similarly, the famous breastplate which Moses was instructed to make, consisted of twelve stones set in four rows. These were called: sardius, topaz, carbuncle; emerald, sapphire, diamond; ligure, agate, amethyst; and finally, beryl, onyx and jasper.

IVORY

' If I were Lord of Tartary,
Myself and me alone,
My bed should be of ivory,
Of beaten gold my throne '.
Tartary
Walter de la Mare

FROM THE TIMES of great antiquity ivory held a great fascination for man. In early cultures when travel and transport were extremely difficult, it was prized as highly as gold or precious stones. Its origin, as a part of an almost mythical animal, was mysterious; it was rare and it had two outstanding qualities. The first was the whiteness of its colour, symbolising purity, and the second was the extraordinary hardness of its substance which the Christians later compared to the incorruptibility of the body of Jesus in the tomb and to the quality of moral fortitude. It is very likely that it was this symbolic idea that inspired the carving of ivory into crucifixes.

Perhaps the most important quality of ivory is its unchangeability. Gold and silver can be recast or melted down and precious stones easily reset, but ivory once carved, cannot be altered. This factor exerted a most formidable influence on ancient art movements. As carved ivory changed hands and travelled from country to country, it inspired new art forms and sculptures of great aesthetic value.

There existed a curious fantasy concerning ivory and in the seventeenth century Sir Thomas Browne refers to it in his writings. All our dreams were believed to pass through a gate made either of horn or of ivory. Those that entered through the ' gate of ivory ' were deluding ones, but those that crossed the ' gate of horn ' always came true.

PEARL

'For truth is precious and divine, —
Too rich a pearl for carnal swine'.
Hudibras
Samuel Butler

MYSTERIOUSLY concealed in an oyster shell, the pearl represents a 'mystic centre' shrouded in obscurity, or the human soul more precious than the body which contains it. An ancient Vedaic hymn is a eulogy to the sacred power of the pearl, 'born of heaven, born of the sea'. It says: 'the bones of the gods are turned to pearl; they take life and move in the bosom of the waters. So I put thee on for life, vigour and strength, for the life of a hundred autumns. May the pearl protect thee'!

Among the Chinese the pearl was an emblem of fertility and an oyster, which contains the yin principle only, was said to help childbirth. The Greeks and the Romans, who were much given to wearing amulets studded with every kind of gem, also considered that the pearl had occult powers and brought luck in love and marriage. The use of the pearl in medicine

as a cure for madness, fever or jaundice, could only have come from the magic and religious importance it held in earlier times. But with the arrival of Christianity it became also a symbol of salvation. In the New Testament Jesus says: 'The Kingdom of Heaven is like unto a merchant man, seeking goodly pearls; who when he found a pearl of great price, went and sold all that he had, and bought it'.

As an emblem of truth the single pearl has had a deep symbolic significance but as an object of wealth it has often been the centre of extravagant and ostentatious display. Cleopatra is said to have drunk a pearl 'dissolved' in a cup of wine to impress Mark Antony, while Thomas Gresham consumed one worth fifteen thousand pounds in honour of Elizabeth I at the opening of the Royal Exchange.

EGG

'A hen is only an egg's way of making another egg'.
Life and Habit
Samuel Butler

THE FUNDAMENTAL mystery of life lies within the egg which is born of a seed, is a seed itself and, therefore, a symbol of rebirth in the animal world, as well as the universe. That the world was egg-shaped, was believed by many civilisations. The myths of the Chinese, Hindus and particularly the Egyptians are based on this idea, claiming that the world was hatched from an egg laid by the Great Creator, whatever his identity. The Egyptians venerated the god Ra as the hope of eternal life, and he was frequently represented still surrounded by the egg from which he had originally emerged. The Orphic myth of creation, however, tells that the union of the Great Goddess and the Snake Ophion hatched the Universal Egg and produced the god Apollo. Since snake eggs are normally hatched by the sun, Apollo became associated with the sun and its orbit.

Alchemy probably originated in early Egypt and possibly the idea of a hidden life, later becoming the occult, stemmed from the mystery of the egg. Since in alchemy any fluids like blood, water and sperm were believed to contain life, the yolk and the white of an egg were also the perfect fluids of life and immortality, matter and thought.

The cock was the Orphic bird of resurrection, sacred to the son of Apollo, whose name was Aesculapius and who was a famous physician with a reputation for restoring the dead to life. Consequently, with time, the snake's egg was replaced by that of a hen, particularly among the Druids, whose festival of Spring was a great event. The egg was coloured red in honour of the sun and so began the tradition of coloured eggs at Easter.

Pliny records some interesting facts about the fabled Druid's Egg. He claims that he had one in his possession and that it was hatched by several serpents who then kept it in the air with their hissing. The person who was able to catch this buoyant egg and avoid being struck by the snakes had to be very agile, for the venom of these creatures was deadly. The egg had magic powers, which could make its owner very rich and win all contests. This idea is probably the basis of the fairy tale of the 'Goose that laid the Golden Egg'.

When an egg has been eaten, to break the shell is a common habit. Although the origins of this practice have been lost, it is certain that the Romans used to break their empty egg shells in order to prevent their enemies from making magic with them. There has always been a very strong connection between the food which man has eaten and what is left of it. Many primitives believe that by injuring the remains they can injure the consumer of the food.

MILK

' Weave a circle round him thrice,
And close your eyes with holy dread,
For he on honey-dew hath fed,
And drank the milk of Paradise '.
Kubla Khan
Samuel Taylor Coleridge

MILK IS A symbol of fertility, abundance and sometimes purity. It has always been considered an essence of goodness; its absence leading to great hardship and suffering. Figuratively, a land of milk and honey is one which has been blessed by the heavens; into such a land God promised to guide the Israelites out of Egypt. This was also the land of the Golden Race where the subjects of Cronus lived joyfully without labour or care, drinking milk and eating the fruit of the earth. Another myth tells the story of the Milky Way which was made by the spouting milk of the Goddess Rhea after the birth of the infant Zeus.

In primitive magic where fertility rites play one of the most important roles, spells were devised to increase milk in both women and cattle. Jade, when powdered with milk and honey was said to stimulate the flow of milk, as did certain stones when worn as charms. But when the Celtic witches, changed into hares, reputedly sucked the cows dry, other antidotes had to be found. A fire was made from cows' dung and on this a pan filled with milk and pins was boiled. As the pins agitated inside the pan so the witches were pricked all over their bodies, and in their discomfort disclosed their identity, begging for mercy.

During the witch-hunts of the Middle Ages, every witch was thought to own a familiar given to her by the Devil. The familiar was often a toad or a cat, and a witch would feed it with her own milk through a third teat made under her arm by the Devil's pincers. Such marks were searched for and often condemned an innocent to death.

SALT

' Thou shalt make proof how the bread of others
savours of salt, and how hard a path is the
descending and the mounting of another's stairs '.
Divine Comedy. Paradiso
Dante Alighieri

SALT IS synonymous with strength and superiority. In his Sermon on the Mount, Christ refers to his disciples as ' the salt of the earth ', or the best and most perfect of mankind. Similarly, in the Talmud, salt symbolises the Torah, for as a world cannot exist without salt, so it cannot without the Torah. This idea gave rise to the custom of ' sitting above salt ', meaning to sit in a place of honour or superiority. This term is literal as each family used to own a massive silver salt cellar, always placed in the middle of the table. Important and distinguished guests sat between the salt and the heads of the family, while the inferior guests and the dependants were seated below it.

Since salt is often used to protect food from decay, it is a purifying agent and a symbol of incorruptibility. The promise made to Aaron by God, concerning the children of Israel, is therefore called a ' covenant of salt ' in the Bible and held sacred in perpetuity. Similarly,

among the Arabs, it was an unwritten law that once salt had been shared, an everlasting bond of friendship was created and could not be severed by the guest or host. As an emblem of purity, salt was often used by the Jews as well as the Greeks and Romans in their religious sacrifices. Even now it is used by the Catholic Church in preparation of holy water since, traditionally, salt is detested by Satan.

The magical properties of salt are believed in by all primitives and it is a very potent ingredient in casting spells. Thrown after a victim, it causes him terrible irritation and unrest so that he cannot sleep by night and must wander by day. Because salt is stimulating, it is connected with sex and often takes a major place in rituals preceding marriage. When mixed with love potions it serves to arouse passion and when sprinkled into the hair of the beloved, it will draw him physically near.

OIL

' In virtues nothing earthly could surpass her,
Save thine ' incomparable oil ', Macassar '!
Don Juan
Lord Byron

THROUGHOUT the ages, oil has been known for its soothing properties and used in almost every purification rite. The Christian church accepted it as a symbol of the Grace of God and still uses it in the sacraments of baptism and ordination.

One of the commonest Assyrian forms of divination was by pouring oil on water and determining future events by the patterns it made. The building of palaces and temples was only undertaken after consulting such oracles. Bede, in his *Ecclesiastical History* written in 731 A.D., tells the story of St Aidan who gave a cruse of oil to pour on stormy waters to a company of people crossing the sea. Their lives were saved, but whether this was due to the sanctity of the oil or the fact that large quan-

tities of it do decrease the violence of waves is not mentioned.

There are countless references to the use of oil in magic. Hecate, a goddess of magic, and her priests practised extreme chastity and in preparation for rituals anointed their bodies with fragrant oils. The Karcists, when practising white magic, sprinkled themselves with oil of olive, myrrh, cinnamon and galingale. And in the Middle Ages, those possessed by the Devil were exorcised with the help of holy oil. An elephant hunter in Africa, however, fears the magical properties of oil. When he goes out to hunt, he forbids his wife to cut her hair or oil her body in his absence. For if she does this, the elephant is certain to break the nets and slip out of the trap.

MAN

MAN IS A unique being who contains within himself the symbolism of the entire universe in miniature. He is the sun, the moon and the stars, and all that is of earth. Whether man has been created in the image of God or whether God had to be invented in the image of man is relatively unimportant. All religions confirm the divine essence of man; because he is conscious of being man and godly, he must be regarded as a symbol. This belief is the basis of magic, the Cabala and every oriental as well as European philosophy. Man can, through learning and meditation, reach the divine state. Even the Greeks and the Romans, in their mythologies, permitted mortals to become demi-gods or gods. Many oriental and more archaic concepts compare the flesh and bones of man to earth; his breath to air; body-heat to fire; and blood to water, stressing the four elements. In ancient astrology we also find the idea of the body relating to the universe, and here the head becomes the heavens, breath is air, the belly is the waters, and the legs and the genitals refer to the earth.

In the theory of numbers, man also appears as a symbol of the universe. According to Pythagoras, the world was built upon the power of numbers, and the division of man into five equal parts probably originated with the Hebrews and the Greeks. This divine number, in relationship to the body, is used in magic, suggested by the pentagram, and related to the five wounds of Christ. We have five senses, four limbs and a head, and the hand has five fingers. On a more esoteric level, the Cabala says that the number nine, or the multiple of three by three, is the essence of the power of man. The number three also appears in the teachings of the Taoists in the far East; the divisions being, the body, the life and the spirit. The three further distinctions of each are qualified by the active, passive and neutral factors.

Inevitably, the position of the human body can also have a great symbolic meaning, since it can express spiritual progress and evolution. Man lying down is at rest and in a passive state; man standing up implies action and life. The attitude of extended arms and legs, together with the head, forms a five-pointed star. The arms and legs alone form an X which, like the hour glass, is related to the union of the world and the soul. A figure with extended arms only, is in the shape of a cross and can be identified with the crucifixion, also as a source of union between earth and heaven, or between death and resurrection.

There is an old legend that man was originally bisexual, but the Jewish lore says that Adam was male on his right side and female on his left, and that God separated the two. This legend justified the existence of the two sexes with the idea that man was created in the image of God. In modern psychology the left side of man symbolises the unconscious and the right is the side of consciousness. The ancient art of alchemy represented man and woman by sulphur and mercury, and the product of the two was the Metal. Similarly, the union of man and woman, the conscious and the unconscious, or the left side and the right, leads to a divine state of being.

HEART

'A good heart is better than all the heads in the world'.
The Disowned
Edward Bulwer Lytton

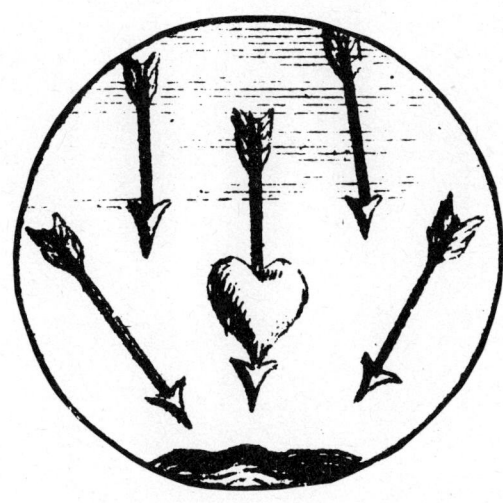

PLATO LOCATED the soul of man in the heart and made it the ruler of the emotions and the intelligence. The three most important points of a human being are the mind, the heart and the genitals. Because the heart is placed in the middle, it becomes a centre from which everything unfolds, and around which, like the axis on a wheel, everything revolves. Venerated by the Hebrews and later the Christians, the heart was a symbolic source of love, courage, devotion and understanding. The *Book of Samuel* says: 'for man looketh on the outwards appearance, but the Lord looketh on the heart'. For the alchemist the heart was the image of the sun within man. And since to love means to be drawn towards a specific centre, the union of the heart and the sun, as expressed by Cupid and his arrow, became a symbol of love.

As the heart also implies eternity, it was the only organ left in a mummified body to ensure its immortality. Among the texts of the *Egyptian Book of the Dead,* there is a drawing of a man standing before a set of balances, looking at his heart which is being weighed against a feather, the symbol of righteousness. The most evil sorcery of those ages was to deprive a man of his heart. But the Christians adopted the emblem as their own and it became the attribute of Jesus and a great many saints. The flaming heart suggests religious fervour, but when it is pierced by an arrow, it symbolises contrition, repentance and devotion under great trial. The heart with a cross on it is a special symbol of St Catherine of Siena and legend says that Christ did one day appear to her and replaced her heart with his own. Renaissance art frequently personified abstract ideas. Among the Seven Virtues, for instance, Charity is often shown as a woman holding a heart in her hand, with children playing around her.

BLOOD

' And if our blood alone
Will melt this iron earth,
Take it. It is well spent
Easing a saviour's birth '.
Tempt Me no More
Cecil Day Lewis

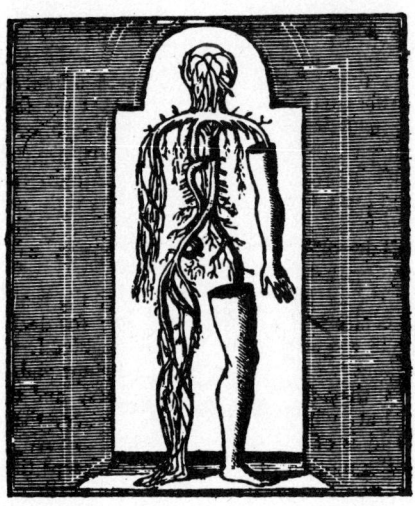

A POWERFUL symbol of life, blood is a vital force, the offering of which appeases the gods. All sacrifices of liquids such as honey, milk or wine offered in ancient times, were images of blood, the most precious gift of all. Many mythological references to animal sacrifices and the story of Christ, who shed his own blood to redeem mankind from sin, express the importance of blood as a means of warding off harm and evil. In alchemy, blood was used in the creation of the Stone because it infused it with the energy of life. The Catholic mass still transforms the bread and wine into the body and blood of Christ.

The blood of an executed man, dying in full health, anger and vitality, protects others from all misfortunes. People struggled for the blood of Charles I and Louis XVI at their executions; the stained rags and handkerchiefs were used against disease and evil. A classical cure for epilepsy was to drink the blood of a killed gladiator, which would also revitalise a weak body.

Blood is associated very closely with its own red colour, which contains a quality of passion and signifies violence and danger. Mars was the god of bloodshed and war, and astrology connects his planet with red. Primitive natives, and even the early chiefs of Rome, painted their bodies red for battle; red like blood, being regarded a source of energy and vitality. Red is also the light over a brothel, connecting the colour with sexuality. For his great vigour and a fierce temper, David in the *Book of Samuel* was known as a ' man of Blood '. Today, red is a danger signal. It stands for rebellion, action, love, victory and shame, expressing violent emotions.

HEAD

' Uneasy lies the head that wears a crown '.
King Henry IV
Shakespeare

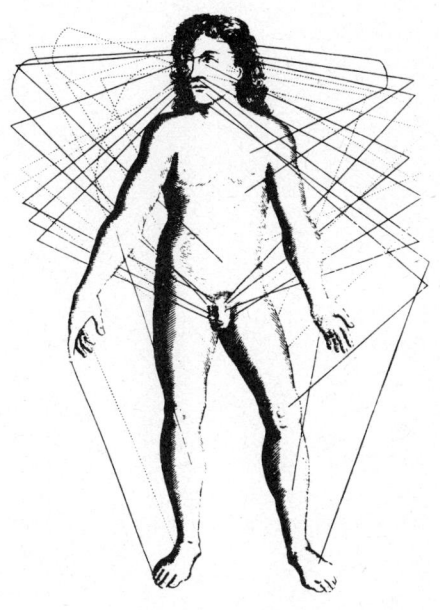

THE HEAD, AS the most important part of the body, is used often to represent the whole man. In mediaeval art, it is a particular symbol of spiritual life and of the mind. Christ became the spiritual head of his church, not only because of his great influence, but also for giving eternal life and strength to his disciples. Two or three-headed creatures exist in astrology and in some mythologies. The dual nature of Gemini and of the two-faced Roman Janus reinforce the symbolic meaning of the head; but Hecate, the goddess of the underworld, was always shown with three heads, possibly relating to her evil powers on earth, in heaven and in hell.

The Egyptian magician was credited with the power of restoring severed limbs and even heads, while among the Hebrews, the mummified head of a first-born child was used in divination. It was an ancient practice to cast oracles with the skull; placed beside a sleeping person, it was supposed to whisper of future events during the night. Human heads, or imitations made of brass were placed on hand-made golden platters, to be consulted on special occasions. Even the Bible refers to the severed head of John the Baptist, carried also on a platter by Salome, following some ancient Hebrew tradition or ritual.

The head is considered very sacred in many parts of the world. In Java, Malaya and Cambodia, it possess a spirit which is holy and must be respected. To touch a Cambodian's head is an insult. Many of them will not enter a room which has something suspended above head level. For the same reason, their houses are built in a single storey so that no neighbour can live over their heads.

HAIR

' Bobby Shaftoe's fat and fair,
Combing down his yellow hair;
He's my love for evermore,
Pretty Bobby Shaftoe '.
Nursery Rhyme
Anonymous

THE LONG HAIR and beard of a man is associated with great virility, strength and powers of wisdom. Since the head is a symbol of higher functions and the seat of the spirit, long hair adds to this symbolic image. But a hairy body refers to the baser part of human nature, and the shaggy, goat-like limbs of the Devil, marked him an evil and inferior being. Cutting the hair leads to weakness, loss of power and great humiliation, as in the story of Samson and Delilah. In the Middle Ages, the witch was shaved before her trial; today men in prison have short cropped hair. Yet in many traditions, a shaved head indicates asceticism and a total devotion to the spirit. With a holy vow given to God, the hair becomes a ritual offering of the natural vitality and energy possessed by man.

Ancient Egyptians sometimes depilated their entire bodies. Many tweezers, razors and combs unearthed through archeological excavations, proved that the people were very particular about cleanliness and coolness. But for public appearances the Egyptian kings, and even Queen Hatshepsut, wore false beards held down by straps. Both men and women dressed in elaborate wigs, a custom which was later adopted in Europe at the court of the bald Louis XIII. From the seventeenth century onwards, the wig was associated with wealth, prestige and professional status. Traditionally, the Speaker of the House, barristers and judges still wear wigs. Hair that is loose and flowing, however, has also signified penitence since the arrival of Christianity. This meaning may have come from the story of the woman who had sinned and begged for the forgiveness of Jesus, by washing his feet with her tears, and wiping them with her hair.

The single tuft on a bald head also had its specific origins. The ancients believed that unless a lock of hair was given to Proserpine, the goddess of the underworld and the wife of Pluto, she would refuse to release the soul from the dying body. The Moslems shaved their heads leaving one tuft, for Mohammed to grasp when pulling the dying man into Paradise. The North American Indians had a similar custom but for more practical reasons. A lock of hair was left on the head, so that the victorious enemy could hold it when cutting the scalp of his victim.

BREATH

' Each person is born to one possession which
outvalues all his others — his last breath '.
Pudd'nhead Wilson
Mark Twain

THE ACCUMULATION and release of breath has a natural rhythm like the waxing and waning of the moon, or the ebb and flow of the tides. These rhythms are universal and fundamental to nature and the cosmos, and through this comparison the symbolism of breath is best expressed. Breathing exercises in Yoga, which lead to greater control of the body and mind, are in imitation of these patterns and aim at greater harmony with the world. Not only is air absorbed through breathing, according to this theory, but also vital energy and life force called ' prana ' in Sanskrit. The alchemists considered it a solar light and maintained that ' we breathe this astral gold continuously '.

In primitive societies, ancient beliefs are often greatly magnified. Among the Maori, it was believed that the breath of the chief was so sacred that it could cause instant death. He was never permitted to blow on fires, as the holy breath could taint the timber with power enough to destroy anyone who then handled it. The soul of a king was also thought to be released through his last dying breath. For this reason the contenders for the throne would crowd the bedside, waiting to catch this breath by mouth or in a bag. The ingenuity used to gain the succession was incredible. Only ardent faith and greed could have prompted one candidate to bore a hole in the floor where the king was lying face down and thus seize his soul and throne through a bamboo tube.

EYE

' Then we shall rise
And view ourselves with clearer eyes
In that calm region where no night
Can hide us from each other's sight '.
Exequy on the Death of a Beloved Wife
Henry King, Bishop of Chichester

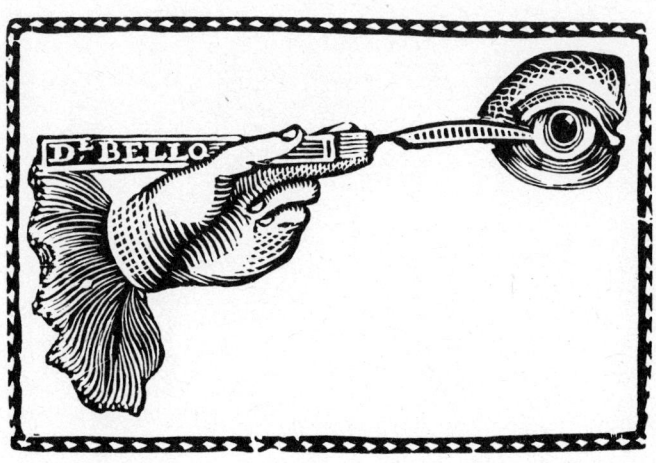

THE SENSE OF sight was a subject of great controversy between the schools of Ancient Greece. Some thought that the eye gave out rays, others believed that the object seen affected the eye. Plato finally concluded that at least three processes had to occur simultaneously. The eye had to emit a divine fire which united with the solar light and the rays of the viewed object; all these factors combined, enabled us to see. These ideas also essentially relate to the meaning of the eye. If we consider the sun as a source of light, and assume that light is symbolic of deep understanding and of spiritual value, then the eye itself must be a symbolic part of the body. Egyptians described the ' divine eye ' by representing the pupil of the eye as a sun and the iris as a mouth which contained it. This sign is like the symbol of the Holy Trinity, shown as the ever present and all-knowing eye of God set in a triangle.

Although one eye is a symbol of great perception, many eyes express inferiority. In Greek mythology, the single eye in the centre of the Cyclops' forehead gave him powers superior to those of ordinary human beings; but Argus who had one hundred eyes to protect him, could not escape death at the hands of Hermes The mediaeval devil was painted with eyes all over his body, and here they marked him as a dissolute being. Another interpretation of these eyes was that they represented a star-lit night. Ironically, he was left in a state of darkness.

Christianity also made the eye a symbol of enevy and desire. Jesus himself said: ' If thy right eye offend thee, pluck it out '. Eye disease caused by dust and germs, and the glare of the sun, plagued the people of Biblical times and blindness was attributed to sin.

EAR

'And if the servant shall plainly say . . .
I will not go out free: . . . his master
shall bore his ear through with an aul;
and he shall serve him for ever '.

Book of Exodus
The Bible

TO THE HEBREWS, the ear was symbolic of possession, and a pierced ear the sign of ownership. But the Assyrians and Egyptians, according to ancient drawings and carvings, used the ear to display their wealth. The ear was shown ornamented with gold and precious stones, sometimes in the form of amulets, to protect them from witchcraft and evil. The earliest Christian reference is to the story of Simon Peter who drew his sword at the arrest of Jesus and cut off the ear of the servant of Caiaphas. In this sense, the ear became a symbol of betrayal and the Passion, and the old practice of cutting off the ear for criminal offences may have been a continuation of this tradition.

Whispering galleries, such as the one still existing beneath Hastings Castle, served to overhear the conversation of prisoners. These chambers were cut from solid rock and connected by underground passages to the king's palace, where the listening post was shaped like an ear. The most famous of these, Dionysius's Ear, was in Syracuse.

A superstition dating back to ancient times is the tale that the ear tingles if someone talks about us in our absence. The source is untraceable, although both Pliny and Shakespeare refer to it. Sir Thomas Browne does say, however, that there was a belief that our guardian angels always touched their right ears if the talk was good, and the left if unfavourable.

HAND

' Even there shall they hand lead me,
and thy right hand shall hold me '.
Psalm 139
The Bible·

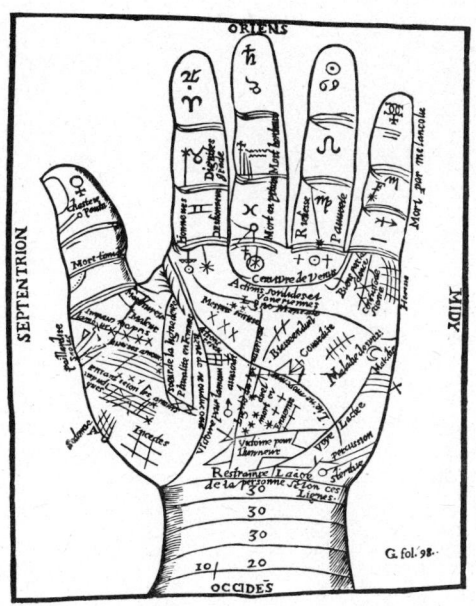

IN THE LANGUAGE of ancient Egypt, the word for hand was related to the word for pillar, expressing support, force and strength. For the Romans, the hand meant also protection and authority, and sometimes appeared instead of the eagle, surmounting the emblems of the imperial legions. Early Christians hesitated to paint God figuratively, so He was often represented by a hand emerging from a cloud, a sign of His protection and His omnipotence. As a symbol, the hand has acquired its meanings from the many gestures that are used instead of words. The simple handshake of friendship probably arose from the imploring hand of the weaker, outstretched towards the stronger. Fashion and custom extended this emotional display to bowing and kissing of the hand, still used as a mark of respect in religious and royal circles. The Biblical references to hand gestures are many, and the meaning of most of these has survived. To wash one's hands conveys innocence; to stretch out the hand is to invite; to lift it up against someone is to rebel; to give it is to promise or unite.

Jung suggests that the symbolism of the hand lies in its power to produce and create. Men possessing certain spiritual gifts ordained and consecrated priests, judges and magistrates, by the laying on of hands. The hand of Jesus and of many others, practised the art of healing. Mesmer called this power a magnetic force, using his hands as does the modern hypnotist. The reverse was true among other races such as the Polynesians. There the hands of kings and chiefs were taboo, because the mysterious forces emanating from them could have contaminated others on contact.

The importance of the left and right hand is now almost lost, but the Biblical seat of honour, whether for the guest or the favourite son, was on the right hand side. The Greek legend of Cronus says that he castrated his father, Uranus, by grasping his genitals with the left hand and that it has ever since remained the hand of ill-omen. The symbolism of the left is that of the unconscious, mysteriouse and sinister, whereas that of the right is rational, conscious and virile.

Although linked hands can express union and strength, the Romans also felt that clasped hands thwarted the free course of things and impeded action; comparing this attitude to knots tied of thread or rope. No man was allowed to cross his legs or hands at sacrifices, war councils or important meetings. Mythology records that Alcmena was in labour with Hercules for a very long time. This was because the goddess of childbirth, Lucina, was found sitting in front of the house and her hands were clasped. The child could not be born until she was persuaded to change her position.

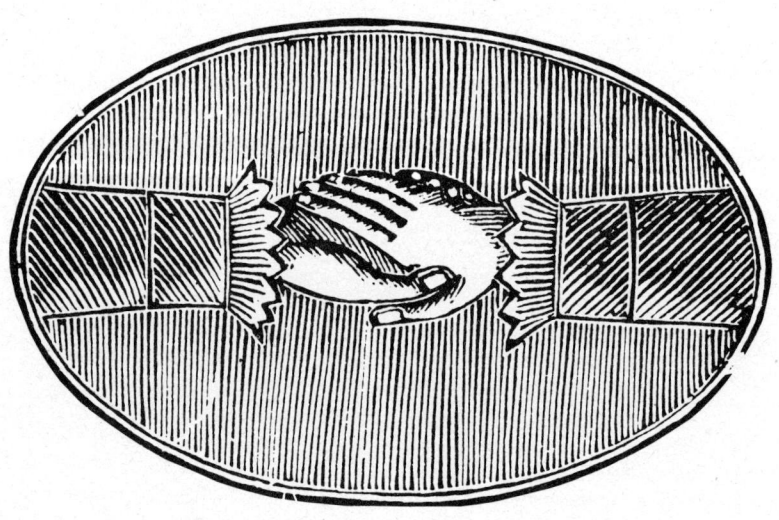

FOOT

' Go, and catch a falling star,
Get with child a mandrake root,
Tell me, where all past years are,
Or who cleft the Devil's foot '.
Song
John Donne

BECAUSE THE foot supports a man upright, it is considered to be symbolic of the human soul. This idea is implied in a Celtic myth of Math, the son of Mathony, king of North Wales. Math's virtue was placed in his feet and, except in time of war when he had to ride into battle, they were always kept in the lap of a royal footholder. This custom survived until mediaeval times and suggests that the foot of a king or god, like his soul, was once believed to be vulnerable. The theme is repeated in the myth of Achilles, whose heel was pierced by Paris's arrow and in the story of Talus, whose heel was injured by Medea's pin. Lameness in Greek legends was a defect which carried with it a compensating gift. Hephaestus, with his twisted feet, excelled in the art of working metals and built palaces for the gods on Mount Olympus. The cloven foot of the Devil, was a mark of his evil genius, while the poet Byron was described by Macaulay as having ' a head which statuaries loved to copy, and a foot the deformity of which the beggars in the streets mimicked '.

The ancient slave walked barefoot and this is probably why the Christians accepted the foot as a symbol of humility. An essential part of the body, the foot is in contact with reality and the earth. By association, the footprint has acquired deep significance. The Danes always concluded their treaties with a pledge of fidelity, sprinkling each other's footprints with their own blood. Pythagoras forbade damaging a man's footprints, for if the soul lay in the feet, then tampering with the footprint also injured its owner. A similar idea existed among the primitive hunters who, by mutilating the animal spoors, ensured the killing of their prey.

BONE

' Good friend, for Jesu's sake forbear
To dig the dust enclosed here.
Blest be the man that spares these stones,
Cursed be he that moves my bones '.
Shakespeare's *Epitaph*

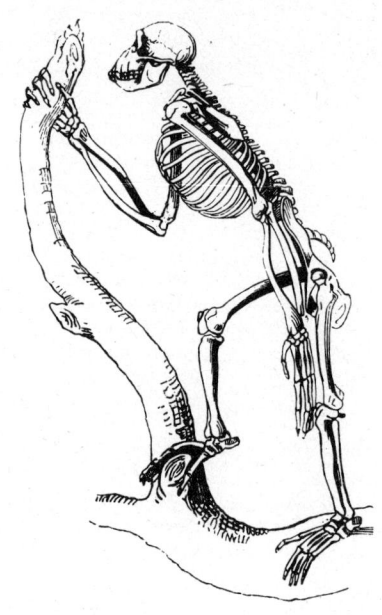

BONE, VIRTUALLY indestructible after death, is a symbol of the resurrection. Although this is one of the reasons that the Roman Catholic Church still resists cremation, the evidence of this symbolic meaning is found mostly in primitive societies. The Zulus believe that the bone of a very old animal can restore their health, allowing them to live for as long as the animal itself. The medicine men of other African tribes claim to be able to bottle up a departing soul in hollow bones, and so return it to its owner. As an emblem of death, the skull and crossbones is the pirate's flag, while the Australian aborigine still places a death curse on his enemy by pointing a bone.

The bone has many magical properties. The aboriginal man constructs deadly charms from the bones of animals or birds eaten by an enemy, while he is quick to hide the remains of his own meal. To ensure good crops, the human bone is also used by the witchdoctor to control rain. In some parts of the world, the bones of the dead are joined into a skeleton and hung in a cave. When water is poured over the skeleton, it is believed that the spirit of the dead collects it, converts it into rain and permits it to fall from the sky. In pre-war China, it was thought that unburied human remains could feel the ill effects of rain. When corpses were exposed, counter charms had to be performed for dry weather and then the crops failed. To prevent famine, the Chinese authorities had to make sure that no human bone was left unburied.

ANIMALS

AS A RELIGIOUS symbol, the animal was found in both primitive totemism and through excavation of early historical objects. Animals were worshipped for their distinguishing characteristics of shape, movement, colour and their relationship to man. Because an animal is of a less complex nature than man, it can be classified according to certain qualities it possesses. The most fundamental division associates all warm-blooded mammals with fire, birds with air, reptiles with earth and every aquatic and amphibious animal with water.

From the Sumerians we inherit tiny, incised seals decorated with patterns; always the animals motif outnumbers the others. The Egyptians honoured animals so extensively that most of their gods were represented with the head of some animal. Hathor, the goddess of love, was usually represented with the head of a cow, for example, and Set's head was often that of a donkey. The horse was a symbol of Persia, as the lion was of Babylon, and sacred bulls were buried within the huge sarcophagi in the Serapeum of Memphis. In Roman art the wolf, bull, lion and wild boar occurred frequently and the symbolic meaning of such animals is reached by analogy. The bear, for instance, represented both strength and cruelty.

Much later the system of watermarking paper spread into the western world. From the thirteenth century onwards, we have evidence of the pig, cat, camel, leopard or griffin making an appearance in this form, and this practice no doubt had mystic and occult origins. In modern times it is interesting to consider the vision of animals seen by painters such as Chagall or Douanier Rousseau, since according to Jung, animals in dreams express the most primitive instincts of our unconscious.

LION

' And there the lion's ruddy eyes
Shall flow with tears of gold ' . . .
Songs of Innocence
William Blake

THE LION IS TO the earth what the eagle is to the sky and these strong and virile opponents are each the rulers of their kingdoms. The symbol of the lion is one of the oldest and richest in meaning and its relationship to gold and the sun has made it the emblem of gods and kings. In alchemy, gold was called the ' lion of metals ' and was the masculine principle of vigour and strength. In astrology, the lion together with gold, is ruled by the sun and affects the heart and the spine; the centres of courage and force. A young lion can be compared to the rising sun at dawn, and an old lion to the setting sun at the end of the day.

The Phoenicians personified the lion as Ruti, and the Egyptian Bast, goddess of solar warmth and fertility, was originally a lioness who only later assumed the body of a lesser cat. Portrayed with the head of a lioness was Sekhmet the ' Powerful ', a terrible lady of war whose ' heart rejoiced when she slew men ', and her son, Nefertum, often appeared standing on a lion. The Egyptians thought that the animal was sacred and responsible for the annual flooding of the Nile since this occurred in July and August when the sun is in the sign of Leo. The Greeks and the Romans adopted the idea and decorated their fountains with lion heads from whose mouths poured streams of water. In honour of the Babylonian Ishtar, sixty colourfully glazed lions adorned the wall leading to the Temple of Marduk, and Ishtar herself was represented bow in hand, on a chariot drawn by seven lions.

Hercules, like Samson, wrestled with a lion

and strangled it with his bare hands, freeing the Nemean valley from the menacing beast. The golden pelt he carried with him miraculously made him invulnerable to bronze, iron and stone. The Phrygian Cybele, whose cult was early introduced into Greece, revenged herself on the thoughtless lovers Hippomenes and Atalanta whom she changed into lions and enslaved for ever at her side.

In Palestine the lion has been extinct since mediaeval times, but it frequently appears in the Bible and is metaphorically paired with the lamb to form a symbol of peace. An old legend has it that lion cubs are born dead and only come to life after three days when breathed upon by their sire. To the Christians this became the perfect allegory of the resurrection and Jesus was called 'The Lion of the tribe of Judah'. For great courage, the emblem was also acquired by Richard I, and since Philip I, Duke of Flanders, adopted it as his own device, the lion has figured in heraldry. Earthbound or winged, the lion symbolises regal dignity, the struggle against evil, and victory.

BEAR

' And behold another beast, a second,
Like to a bear, and it raised up itself
on one side, and it had three ribs in the
mouth of it between the teeth of it '.

Book of Daniel
The Bible

THE SYMBOLISM of the bear as all that is primitive, crude and cruel, seems to have existed from the earliest times. In spite of the great dangers involved, Neanderthal man, some seventy thousand years ago, went out of his way to hunt it down, although easier prey was plentiful. There is no doubt that ritual sacrifice was involved, as several caves have been discovered containing bear skulls placed on altar-like structures. Modern primitives, from the North American Indian to the Ainu of Japan or the Orochon of Siberia, still take part in the bear-hunt, considering the animal sacred and in direct contact with their gods. The myths of the Haida Indians on the Pacific Coast tell of a whole tribe of Bear People, and these creatures have been the inspiration of some of the finest Indian art of that region.

The bear is also the most common totemic symbol in practically every part of the world where it lives. To the Lapps it is the King of the Beasts and to kill it is the height of glory, provided that the taboos are strictly observed as any sacrilege could bring fatal results.

In Greek mythology Artemis, daughter of Zeus, had a she-bear as her symbol. Arcadia, a savage and mountainous region, was her favourite hunting place and in this sport she was followed by her virgin nymphs, and competed with her brother Apollo. But Zeus desired one of her nymphs called Callisto, and despite her vow of chastity she succumbed to his attentions. When Artemis discovered this deceit, Zeus tried to save Callisto by changing her into a bear, but it was already too late, for Artemis had pierced her with an arrow as

48

she was giving birth to Zeus's son. From that time on, Callisto and her child were set up in the sky as the Great and Little Bear by Zeus. Much later, the cult of Artemis continued in Athens, and a legend tells that one day a bear attacked a young girl and her brother was forced to kill it. The bear goddess was so enraged that she sent a deadly plague upon all the Athenians, until they atoned for the deed by consecrating their girl-children to the temple of Artemis every five years.

In the Old Testament we have the story of the two bears, sent by God out of the forest to eat the children who dared to mock the baldness of the prophet Elisha. The corrupt and evil kingdom of Persia, destroyed by God, was also represented by a bear, so the animal symbolised destruction as well as punishment. The Christians, however, used the image of the bear in still another way. In their legend, all bear cubs are born without shape and their mother gives them form some time later. This symbolised the way that the Church remoulded all heathens, giving them a new structure for life.

APE

' There was an Ape in the days that were earlier;
Centuries passed, and his hair became curlier;
Centuries more gave a thumb to his wrist —
Then he was Man — and a Positivist '.
                              The Positivists
                              Mortimer Collins

THE APE, LONG before Darwin's claim to our descent, generally symbolised the coarser and baser nature of man, darkness and unconscious activity. In Christian art the figure of an ape signified sin, lust, malice, cunning and greed — and sometimes Satan himself. This particular symbolism of the ape is strongly Christian in idea since the sense of sin and retribution was much encouraged and emphasised within the Church. If the ape is also symbolic of the primitive forces of the unconscious, these forces need not be necessarily degrading or sinful. In other cultures the reverse was often true. In China, the ape frequently played the role of the sprite or the fairy of the western folktale and could bring health, success and good fortune.

To the Egyptians the ape was even more significant. He was Thoth or sometimes Hapi, later identified with the famous Hermes of the Greeks. He often appeared as a sacred baboon although he also liked to assume the head of an ibis on certain occasions. This ambiguity probably arose from the fusion, in very remote times, of two lunar divinities, one representing a bird and the other an ape. Whatever his origin, Thoth was worshipped at Hermopolis as the god of learning and the inventor of writing, science and all art.

HARE

' I am at a loss to know whether it be
my hare's foot which is my preservative, or
my taking of a pill of turpentine every morning '.
Diary
Samuel Pepys

THE HARE WAS a sacred animal in ancient Britain and Pelasgian Greece. It was known to the Egyptians and is still the Great Spirit, father of the race, to the Algonquian Indian. Originally an 'unclean' animal to the Hebrews, it has become a symbol of fertility and sometimes lust, as it is able to conceive when already pregnant. Swift of movement and a good swimmer, the northern hare turns white during the winter months, and its reputation for March madness is due to the fact that March is its rutting time.

There is a feminine quality about the hare and it has always been associated with female royalty or divinity. Boudicca took it into battle against the Romans and it was sacred to the lunar goddess, Hecate, as well as to the Saxon Ostara, after whom Easter was named. The hare is still traditionally said to 'lay' the Easter egg, although now it has become confused with the rabbit. One of the greatest Chinese festivals is that of the moon and the chief object of worship is the hare, who is said to live on the moon and spend its time making the elixir of immortality. This feast is especially for women and children; men never take part in it, as the hare is the symbol of homosexuality and considered to be its patron. Even in Christian art a white hare is sometimes placed at the feet of the Virgin Mary, although here it is symbolic of her triumph over lust.

As a symbol of fertility, the animal is also a common embodiment of the corn spirit. In Gallway the reaping of the last standing patch of corn is called 'cutting the hare'. An effigy of the hare is made by plaiting and knotting

51

the corn and the reapers throw their sickles in an attempt to cut it down. The successful reaper carries it proudly home and hangs it on his door until next year. Similar customs are known all over Europe and are practised to ensure fruitful harvests in the future.

The African primitive was quick to recognise the faintheartedness and the swiftness of the hare. By sympathetic magic, eating its flesh made the warrior cowardly and the hunter's quarry too swiftfooted to be caught. But the meat of the hare was not only taboo in Africa. The scientists and doctors of the Middle Ages considered it would poison anyone who ate it with 'melancholia', a disease from which the hare itself suffered and tried to cure by eating chicory. In spite of this belief, the hare became an allegorical figure for its fleetness and diligence and appears often on Gothic sepulchures and in the art of that period.

ASS

The ass will carry his load, but not a
double load; ride not a free horse to death '.
Don Quixote
Cervantes

THE EARLIEST symbolism of the ass was connected with lust and evil. The wicked god, Set, brother to Osiris, was wild and rough with the pale skin and red hair hateful to the Egyptians, who compared it to the pelt of an ass. The cult of the ass-eared god spread with bloodshed and orgy, later becoming related with demons such as the Empusae who had one leg made of brass while the other was that of a donkey. In legend, the Lilim or the evil descendents of Adam's first wife, Lilith, had the haunches of the animal. The Orphic tradition considered the ass as impure, while the horse was greatly respected. This attitude is still common in Latin countries and particularly in Spain where 'caballero' means a gentleman and 'carajo' is a swear word.

The concept of the ass as a fool or a jester is probably based on the Greek legend of Midas the Phrygian. When asked to judge a musical contest between Apollo and Marsyas, Midas voted against the flute-playing Apollo. In great fury the god punished him with a pair of ass's ears which were made to grow out of his head. In some European folklore the connection between the fool and the ass is very clear, and the dunce's hat is an object of ridicule. In actual fact the ass is a very intelligent animal but tradition proves stronger than reality.

Another common image of the ass is that of the humblest and most patient animal in creation. This idea is Christian in origin and although the ass appears in the Old Testament quite frequently, it is most strongly associated with the nativity and the life of Jesus. According to legend, the dark cross on its shoulders marked the animal for ever when Jesus rode the ass into Jerusalem on Palm Sunday.

FOX

'May the grass grow at your door and the
fox build his nest on your hearthstone.
May the light fade from your eyes, so
you never see what you love '.
Part of a Traditional Wexford Curse

THE TRADITIONAL symbolism of the fox is that of cunning and slyness. In the *Book of Ezekiel,* the Lord reproves the people by saying: ' O Israel, thy prophets are like the foxes of the desert '. In the Middle Ages, the fox was also a disguise for the Devil and together with the cat and the hare, the animal most often associated with witchcraft. This is not surprising as the Celtic tradition was still deeply ingrained, and showed evidence of similar beliefs.

In mediaeval French and German literature, the fox acquired the general name of Reynard and figured in epics which were written at that time, satirizing current life and events. Some of Chaucer's Tales follow this tradition, as does Caxton's *Hystorie of Reynart the Foxe,* translated from the Dutch in 1481. In this book, the claims of Reynard always proved to be grandiose but false. He was the alleged owner of a magic ring with a stone of three colours. The green made the wearer completely invisible, the red made the night into day and the white cured all diseases. Reynard's famous Globe of Glass was, according to the Caxton version, yet another example of his perfidious nature. This was a treasure which Reynard said he had sent to the Queen, so that she could observe all that was going on, no matter how far off. Unfortunately, it never reached her and remained a figment of Reynard's sly imagination.

PIG

THE PIG represents gluttony and sensuality, and throughout history and legend it is linked with either the Devil or the gods. It is a very prolific animal and this earned it the love of Demeter, the Earth Mother, the goddess of fertility and the cultivated soil. The wild pig taught men to plough the earth, as it does itself when scavenging for food with its short, sharp tusks. In gratitude, the Greeks not only portrayed the pig in the arms of Demeter, but also sacrificed it in her name. The pig is known to devour its young and, before becoming a domestic animal, it fed on carrion and corpses found in tombs; these habits made it 'unclean' to the Egyptians, Hebrews and the Phoenicians.

All religions can be paradoxical. To the ancients the unlawful became lawful on special occasions. So the Egyptians sacrificed the pig to the moon and to Osiris once a year and, though hated at all other times, it was eaten with great relish at these mid-winter festivals. It was believed also that leprosy was the result of touching or drinking the milk of a pig and the swineherds, although Egyptian, were the only people excluded from the temples. They were so despised that nobody wanted to go near them and they had to marry within their own caste. Through all folklore there still runs the theme of the princess who is forced to marry a swineherd, only to find that he is really a prince.

The Hebrews were also forbidden to eat the flesh of the pig, but the reason for this was that they wished to separate their people from the pagan Syrians and Canaanites who used it as food and for sacrifice. History shows that an abhored animal has always been sacred at one time, and we know that until the days of Isaiah, many Jews met secretly to feast on mice and pigs in ancient religious rituals.

The Biblical story of the possessed man of Gaderene reflects also the Jewish hatred of the pig, and connects it with the Devil. The evil spirits begged Jesus to cast them into a grazing herd of swine, so that some two thousand animals were hurled from a high precipice into the sea. The five darker marks on the inner side of the swine's forelegs were the blemishes left by the claws of the Devil as he entered the creature. In Christian art the hog represented the demon of sensuality and it accompanied St Anthony Abbot as a tribute to the saint's great powers of exorcism and his triumph over corruption and sin.

CAT

' Cruel, but composed and bland,
Dumb, inscrutable and grand,
So Tiberius might have sat,
Had Tiberius been a cat '.
Poor Matthias
Matthew Arnold

THE ANCIENT association of the cat was with the goddess of the moon. The animal has been known for about five thousands years and its symbolism varies from royal power to the ultimate in evil. The habits and the colours of a cat suggest the different ways in which it was regarded throughout its long existence. It is an animal of the night, its eyes shine in the dark while its colours, differing like the moon, change from white to red to black. It softly walks alone on padded feet and as a domestic animal, it serves little purpose except to hunt mice which are symbols of pestilence.

The Egyptian cat was sacred to the goddess Bast, who was represented as a cat-headed woman holding in her right hand a sistrum and in her left a basket. Her devotees placed the cat in her temples where it was worshipped to such an extent that upon its death it was embalmed and given a royal funeral. The cat, which was easily tamed, entered the domestic lives of the Egyptians, but its sacred cult was so deeply rooted among the people that it reached peaks of absurdity. Diodorus describes how in the case of fire, the people neglected to save their buildings as they were more concerned with the rescue of their animals; and if the animal was killed by accident or malice, the culprit was put to death. When mourning a cat, an Egyptian would not only cut off his own hair, but have the creature mummified and buried in a sacred ground designed for this purpose.

In ancient Rome, the cat was a symbol of liberty as the animal most opposed to restraint. It had its place also in pre-Christian Ireland, where traces of the cult were found in cave-shrines in Connaught. There it was a ' slender, black cat, reclining upon a chair of silver ', similar to the Egyptian cat, which was also small-headed and long-limbed.

With the arrival of Christianity the cat first came to mean laziness and lust, then to represent Satan himself. The black cat became so strongly identified with witchcraft and the dark realms of the Devil, that it was persecuted and ill-treated in every possible way. It was both feared and held in contempt, and many a mediaeval witch-trial was centred around its very existence. Ceremonial bonfires were held to destroy the evil cat, and the last king to participate in such a ritual was Louis XIV, when sackfuls of cats were burned in the streets of Paris. The people joyfully collected the ashes and took them home, in the belief that the witches had been driven away and that good luck would follow.

LAMB

' And now the time returns again:
Our souls exult, and London's towers
Receive the Lamb of God to dwell
In England's green and pleasant bowers '.

Jerusalem
William Blake

IN MANY passages of the Old Testament, the lamb conveys the idea of vicarious suffering expressed through the act of burnt offerings. It was also a sacrificial animal in early Apollonic temples, its blood being used to inspire prophecy and divination, and as such, it signified innocence under persecution. Meekness, submission, and helplessness when attacked by other animals, contributed also to it becoming the favourite symbolism for Christ as the great Redeemer. John the Baptist, according to the gospels, called Jesus ' The Lamb of God, which taketh away the sins of the world ', and as such, the lamb is most frequently represented in Christian art of all periods.

Christian paintings usually show the Holy Lamb, carrying a cross or a pennon of victory, standing on a small hill from which flow four streams of water. The hill is an allusion to the House of God, or the Church, and the four streams are the four Holy Gospels, flowing towards the earth as the Word of God. Occasionally, the lamb in distress also appears in portrayals of Jesus as the good Shepherd, but here it is used to mean the sinner.

DOG

' The more I see of the representatives
of the people, the more I admire my dogs '.
Count d'Orsay
Alphonse de Lamartine

THE SYMBOL of the dog as a faithful companion of man belongs to the ancient Egyptians. The earliest dog was probably the jackal, a desert animal who, vulture-like, despoiled the dead and became transformed into the god Anubis, companion of the human soul to its final judgment. Anubis presided over all funeral rites and was represented as a dark man with the head of a dog, either in the process of embalming a body or later receiving it at the door of the tomb. The Greeks identified Anubis with Hermes, the conductor of souls.

This connection between death and the dog is expressed in many mythologies. Among the favourite subjects of Greek and Etruscan art is that of Hercules carrying the dog, Cerberus, from the Underworld. This monstrous animal was the keeper posted at the gates of Hades and was described as having fifty heads and a voice of bronze. Only Hercules dared to match his strength against him and when Cerberus was finally brought for a moment to the surface of the earth, he infected with his venom certain herbs which remained poisonous for ever.

Pestilence and great heat were also attributed by the Romans to the brightest star in the sky, the Dog-star. The theory was that, when it rose with the sun at the beginning of July, it redoubled the sun's heat so that the crops were ruined. The Dog-star was, of course, Sirius, the faithful dog of Orion who followed his master into the skies when the god took his place there as a constellation.

The dog as a creature of death appears also in the primitive myth of the Mende people of

60

Sierra Leone. In this story the Supreme Being sent out two messages into the world. One was through the dog, telling man that he was immortal, and the other was through the toad, saying that man must die. Unfortunately, the dog, because of his greed, stopped to get some food on the way and the toad was the first to deliver his unhappy message. Since then, the dog has never been forgiven and is always held responsible for the message of death.

The Bible speaks of the dog as an animal of despicable character, the pariah. Then, it was a ferocious scavenger, feared and ' un-clean ', although evidently useful to the shepherds of Edom. The more friendly image of a sheep-dog later earned the dog some trust until it represented fidelity and watchfulness. Christianity appropriated the symbolism of the sheep-dog and used it allegorically as the priest or the disciple guiding a flock of souls. As a symbol of fidelity in marriage the dog often appeared at the feet of women on mediaeval engravings. As time passed, the animal was also shown at his master's feet as a loved and trusted companion of the hunt.

CAMEL

' The Camel's hump is an ugly lump
Which well you may see at the Zoo;
But uglier yet is the Hump we get
From having too little to do '.

Just-So Stories
Rudyard Kipling

THE CAMEL HAS been used as a beast of burden and a means of transport in the Orient for at least thirty centuries. It is symbolic of temperance, probably because it can go without water for great lengths of time and on less fodder than a horse or an ass. Although it was considered an ' unclean ' animal, the Bible refers to it as evidence of great wealth, a sign of royalty and dignity. Job was reputed to have owned three thousand camels, and Solomon received a ' very great train ' of these animals bearing gifts of gold and precious stones from the Queen of Sheba.

Mohammed himself was a camel driver and the animal plays as important a role in Moslem tradition as does the ass in Christianity. When Mohammed had to flee from Mecca, his favourite camel Al Kaswa, knelt down in Koba and refused to move. This was taken to be a sign from God, and Koba, now commemorated with a famous mosque, remained Mohammed's hiding place for several days. Another fabled camel was Al Adha, who performed the journey from Jerusalem to Mecca in four swift bounds. As a reward, he gained a place in paradise among a few other favoured animals.

The well-known reference in the New Testament, that it is easier for a camel to go through the eye of a needle than a rich man to enter the Kingdom of God, is quoted also in the Koran and in the early rabbinical writings; but here an elephant is substituted for the camel.

RAM

'The mountains skipped like rams,
and little hills like lambs'.
Psalm 114
The Bible

THE RAM IS A symbol of strength, creativity and that initial form of energy which determined the course of action when the universe was born. It appears in the cycle of existence or the zodiac, as the first sign of Aries and bursts forth in the image of spring. Since it is connected with the beginning of any cyclic process, in alchemy the start of the Great Work or the making of the Philosopher's Stone could only begin when the sun was in Aries. Astrologically, it also controls the head and the brain as primary sources of physical and spiritual power. In the Middle Ages it was always a prize at wrestling matches and Chaucer refers to this when speaking of his strong miller: 'At wrastlynge he wolde bere awey the ram'.

In Egyptian mythology, Amon was the god with the head of a ram. His horns were curled and he initiated and protected all life, often being called, 'his mother's husband'. Sacred rams were very popular in Egypt and the greatest of them was Ba Neb Djedet who was said to be the incarnation of Osiris. Once a year, however, a ram was killed and its skin was placed on the statue of Amon, identifying it with this god. The ram was mourned as if Amon himself had died and it was buried in a sacred tomb. The royal or divine status of the ram is repeated throughout mythology and the Bible. In the theme of the sacrifice of the son, the ram is the accepted substitute and it was offered instead of Isaac when Abraham sacrificed to the Lord.

RAT

'Anything like the sound of a rat
Makes my heart go pit-a-pat'.
The Pied Piper of Hamelin
Robert Browning

THE RAT IS A symbol of destruction and is strongly associated with death. Although like most animals, it was deified in Egypt, this was probably because of its extraordinary gift of good judgment and its sense of self-preservation. The Bible calls the mouse and the rat an abomination and plagues of these rodents are well known through history and myth, from ancient China and Egypt to most countries in Europe.

One of the less-known legends is that of a Polish prince called Popiel, who invited all his relations to a banquet and poisoned them with wine. He was severely punished for this as he was devoured by thousands of mice which invaded his castle. Another tale is that of the Pied Piper of Hamelin, who agreed to free the town from a plague of rats for a certain reward. This story is of particular interest as it is also symbolic of the connection between music and death. As the Piper played his tune, all the rats followed him out of the town to their destruction, but when the reward was not forthcoming, the children were beguiled by his music and lost for ever. The musician in this case represents our fascination with death, an inexplicable and unconscious force within us.

In Ireland it was believed that rats could be killed by rhyming; both Shakespeare and Ben Jonson refer to this in their works. Seanchan Torpest, the master-ollave of Ireland in the seventh century, discovered this purely by accident when he uttered a rhyming curse on finding that his dinner had been eaten by rats. Immediately, ten rats dropped dead. This story is not unlike the fable of the Pied Piper, for the use of a chanting rhyme is a form of music.

64

BIRDS

THE BIRD or a winged creature of the air, has long been symbolic of the soul and spiritual elevation as opposed to the fixed and material symbolism connected with other animals of the earth. In Egyptian art, the bird was often depicted with a human head, representing a soul flying away from the body after death. The Greeks portrayed concepts such as love and victory through winged sculptures of the human form. Wings also expressed thought, imagination, intelligence and a divine mission, particularly those of the archangels, seraphim and cherubs of the Christian spiritual heirarchy. As a god itself, the bird was usually of a giant size, perhaps an eagle or a swan. For the Hindus, the bird came from the sun; for the North American Indians, it was the 'Supreme Being'. But the interpretation of the bird as a soul, so often found in folklore all over the world, did not always imply sanctity or goodness. There were birds of cunning and evil, such as the owl and raven.

According to Freud, the bird (like the fish) was originally a phallic symbol, but able to transcend its state into a more spiritual act of love. In fairy tales, the lover is often changed into a bird, or the bird is endowed with the gift of speech or song and becomes the messenger of love to man. There is a passage in the *Book of Revelation* describing the fallen Babylon as ' the habitation of devils, and the hold of every foul spirit, and a cage of every unclean and hateful bird ', which presents the bird as a symbol of evil. This was partially due to the Mosaic law which divided all animals into those that were inedible and those suitable as food. Certain species, however, such as the vulture or the lapwing were also condemned for being birds of prey or for their sanctity in the past. As multiplicity is a sign of degeneration in symbolism so, numerous birds, like the Stymphalian flocks destroyed by Hercules, are always connected with wickedness and evil.

RAVEN

' Ghastly grim and ancient Raven
wandering from the Nightly shore —
Tell me what thy lordly name
is on the Night's Plutonian shore '.
The Raven
Edgar Allan Poe

A NOMADIC, black-plumed bird, the raven accompanied many heroes and gods onto the field of battle. It fed on the flesh of the dead and flew high on the Danish standard of Odin, hanging its wings at defeat and soaring if victory was imminent. Two ravens sat also on the shoulders of the god Odin, one called Mind and the other Memory, whispering oracular words and wisdom into his ears. Bran the Blessed had a raven as his prophet and when he lay dying of battle wounds, he asked for his head to be buried on the White Hill of London. The raven must have followed him there, for the presence of the tame birds protecting the British crown at the Tower of London is otherwise unexplained.

In classical times the raven had all the characteristics of Saturn, the evil and sombre bearer of disaster. The day Cicero was murdered by his enemies, a raven entered the great orator's chamber and woke him with his ominous croaking. But in other cultures it was a bird associated with wider cosmic powers and less drastic acts. Its colour was symbolic of the blackness of a fertile soil and the primal darkness from which life appeared. So, for many Indians of the North American continent, the raven was the winged creator of the visible world.

Two legends claim that originally the raven was a white bird. It seems that it became a messenger of Noah during the time of the Great Flood, but when sent out of the ark to look for land, the raven never returned. Since then, in Jewish mythology, the raven's feathers were tarred and its image likened to Satan.

According to Ovid, a raven was responsible for telling Apollo that his beloved nymph, Coronis, was faithless. In great anger, the god shot Coronis with an arrow and, despising the bearer of the tale,

' He blackened the raven o'er,
And bid him prate in his white plumes no more '.

The raven is also a symbol of solitude. The fugitive prophet, Elijah, was fed by a raven at the brook Cherith and for the hermit, St Paul, the bird was a daily bearer of a loaf bread. One of the Chinese imperial emblems is a curious, three-legged, raven-like bird, its legs contained within a solar circle. This image represents the life of the Emperor and each of the three legs correspond to the sun's position at dawn, at noon and at dusk. The emblem also suggests the isolation and solitude of a great man.

GOOSE

' The lazy geese, like a snow cloud
Dripping their snow on the green grass,
Tricking and stopping, sleepy and proud,
Who cried in goose, Alas '.
Bells for John Whiteside's Daughter
John Crowe Ransome

ONCE A MYSTIC and holy bed of Brahma, once the Great Cackler whose egg gave birth to the Egyptian creator of life, the god Ra, the goose now fallen from favour, means a foolish person and appears in nursery books. But it had once graced the temples of the Gallic Mars and its images were carved from mammoth ivory found by the world's deepest Lake of Baikal. To the Chinese it was a symbol of fertility and the Sumerians believed that Gula's chariot flew high when drawn by four of these beautiful white birds. The magic and mystery of our ancestors is no longer ours. They did not know that the goose is a migratory bird, breeding in the coldest and most inaccessible regions of the Arctic. It appeared to them only as a powerful and constant bird, endowed with immortality, a prerogative of the gods.

The Romans recognised the goose as a symbol of providence and vigilance ever since the cackling of a sacred flock had saved the Capitol from the invading Gauls. But the bird was less fortunate for St Martin of Tours whose greatest wish was to remain a hermit. The Church and the people of Tours, however, called him to become their Bishop and as he tried to hide, a noisy goose disclosed his presence and he had to accept the unwanted privilege.

As a lucky omen and a sign of plenty, the goose continued to appear for a long time. In Goldsmith's ale-houses the dice were doubled for its emblem in the ' royal game of goose '; since Queen Elizabeth the Michaelmas table has been laden with the roasted bird; and the golden egg of folklore was laid by the proverbial goose.

OWL

'It was the owl that shriek'd, the fatal bellman,
Which gives the stern'st good-night'.

Macbeth
Shakespeare

AS A BIRD OF the dead sun which passes through the unknown regions of blackness, the owl of the Egyptian hieroglyphs was a symbol of death, cold and night. Broad-headed and large-eyed, it preys treacherously on lesser birds and mice; flying swiftly and silently with eyes shining in the dark. It once bred profusely in Athens and its likeness was stamped on an Athenian coin. But its reputation for wisdom came from being a messenger of the goddess Athene, who surpassed all others with her gift of prophecy in the days of Ancient Greece. According to Homer, the owl lived also on Calypso's island of Ogygia in the company of the oracular sea-crows. Somehow it must have learned their art, for it had its own temple of augury near Surrentum.

In Ireland the roaring of the seas was pro-phetic of the death of kings and the sharp scream of the screech-owl held the same warning. So the soulless demon Lilith, the first wife of Adam, brought death and destruction as the screech-owl upon the Hebrews. As late as the Middle Ages, amulets were made by the Jews to protect themselves against her evil powers.

In a Celtic legend, Blodeuwedd was turned into an owl and became 'hateful unto all birds'. Her treacherous killing of her husband, Llew, had condemned her to live like the secluded bird. Among the leaves of ivy, its favourite plant, the owl is a symbol of the hermit, and Gray in his Elegy says:
' Save that from yonder ivy-mantled tower
The moping owl does to the moon complain
Of such as, wand'ring near her secret bow'r,
Molest her ancient solitary reign .'

71

SWAN

' Over her the swan shook slowly free
The folded glory of his wings, and made
A white-walled tent of soft and luminous shade '.
Leda
Aldous Huxley

A SYMBOL OF the poets, their source of inspiration and the very soul of Virgil and Apollo, the swan is haunting in its beauty and grace of movement. Venus, on seeing the shape of her own white, soft and rounded body reflected in the water, charged that the swan should be her bird; and so it became the poetic image of a desired, nude but chaste maiden. Yet the swan has another implication; its neck strong and long, moving down towards the water, is masculine in intent and the two-fold meaning makes it a symbol of satisfied desire. This strange, hermaphrodite ambivalence of the swan surrounds it with deepest reverence in mythology and with a sense of magic. Both the knight and the virgin take disguise in magic garments of swan feathers; Jupiter flies to Leda or Lohengrin to Elsa; Caer, a Celtic maiden one year and a swan the next, is the seductress of the noble Angus.

The mysterious song of the dying swan, that even Plato and Aristotle believed to be true, is yet another allusion to the satisfaction of desire, even though that desire should be for death. On a royal crest or on the sign of a tavern, the swan is often shown together with a harp, explaining the swan-song even further. The tone of the harp is sad and intense, its music a lament for the suffering on earth. The passionate swan united with this longing-melody is a symbol of a poet's tragic death and the romantic sacrifice of all for art.

EAGLE

'That eagle's fate and mine are one,
  Which on the shaft that made him die
Espied a feather of his own,
    Wherewith he wont to soar so high'.
To a Lady Singing a Song of His Composing
Edmund Waller

ITS BEAK IS a killing hook, its fall is as deadly as a crossbow bolt, and the eagle's talons are sharper than grapnels. It is the emperor of the birds of prey, and the emblem of emperors. The Tartar khans hunted the antelope with the eagle and it sat only on the wrist of kings in the chase of the Middle Ages. It lives on the high mountains and the Roman legions would try to make their winter quarters by an eagle's nest.

From the Pharaohs to the President of the United States, the eagle has been chosen a symbol of power and empire. In mythology, it is the sun, its talons the lightning. Zeus used the eagle to bring thunderbolts to slay the Titans and to eviscerate Prometheus on his rock, chained in agony for giving the terrible gift of fire to men. On the great tree Yggdrasil

that holds the heaven from the earth in the Norse myths, the eagle sits, observing the wars of the heroes. It is the symbol of immortality; as Aeschylus says, the eagle can only be killed by an arrow winged by its own feathers.

In the ancient empires, the eagle was most famous as the rallying point of the Roman legions. Set high on a pole and carried by a centurion, it strode above slaughter. If the pole broke in battle the men would recognise their own eagle and would rally about it for another stand. The defence of the eagles was the pride of the legions; the loss of the eagles the shame of Rome.

Charlemagne took the eagle as the symbol of his new Europe, and afterwards the imperial powers of the West used the emblem, as if they were the legitimate heirs of Rome. The

Hapsburgs, the Romanovs and the Hohen-zollerns all stole the symbol of Caesar, and so did Mussolini and Hitler's Third Reich. The great bird of prey, sometimes double-headed like a two-edged axe, was always the herald of conquest.

Strange then that the eagle should also be the chosen symbol of the infant United States, pledged to peace and democracy. Yet the new nation was born in a struggle against the British Empire and, on its march across the continent, was at war with the Spanish Empire and the Indian nations, although the eagle's feathers in the chief's headdress did not save them. The American eagle is actually the bald-headed eagle, mainly a scavenger, which prefers to feed on dead fish and pirate the food of other birds of prey. As the Dutch proverb says, ' Folly has the wings of an eagle and the eyes of an owl '.

SPARROW

' For the soul of Philip Sparrow,
That was late slain at Carrow
Among the Nunnes Black,
For the sweet soul's sake
And for all sparrow's souls
Set in our bead-rolls,
Pater noster qui
With an Ave Mari '.
The Sparrow's Dirge
John Skelton

A HUMBLE, twittering bird, the sparrow thrives best in the neighbourhood of man. Always plentiful in Asia and in northern Europe, it is a symbol of the poor and the lowly whom God has created and whom He also protects. St Matthew in his Gospel asks: ' Are not two sparrows sold for a farthing? And one of them shall not fall to the ground without your Father '.

Sparrow sacrifices are mentioned in Leviticus and the psalmist honoured the humility of the bird which often nestled near the altars of the temples. Like the dove, the sparrow was also the companion of Venus, the goddess of love; and the Empress of the Tarot holds a sparrow in one hand while the sign of Venus lies at her feet. She is Ceres, Artemis, a Magna Dea of the East; her beauty also a symbol of feminine creation. The Roman poet, Catullus, mourns the death of a sparrow which belonged to his beautiful mistress, Lesbia, and the poem, no doubt, inspired John Skelton's sad lament of *The Sparrow's Dirge*.

An arrow of plebeian origin has pierced the heart of many an invulnerable god and the sparrow who killed Cock Robin may allude to the downfall of Robert Walpole or to the death of the beloved Norse god, Balder.

PEACOCK

' Remember that the most beautiful
things in the world are the most useless;
peacocks and lilies for instance '.

The Stones of Venice
John Ruskin

THE PEACOCK was the favourite bird of noble ladies and, as an emblem of beauty and glory, it appeared not only in their gardens, but also on a Roman coin. Its strutting display of colour matched the vanity and pride of every princess worthy of her name. In some Eastern countries its feather is still a mark of honour, in others it represents the evil eye. The last, undoubtedly alluding to the legendary Argus, the hundred-eyed monster, whose eyes were for ever set into a peacock's tail when he was charmed to sleep and killed by Hermes. The same eyes, forming the beautiful pattern of its wings, are the stars and planets of the Hindu universe and a symbol of the ' all seeing ' powers of the Christian Church.

As a symbol of immortality, the peacock was adopted by the Christians through some confusion with the phoenix. An attribute of St Barbara of Heliopolis, the peacock's feather became the emblem of the city of her birth. But Heliopolis was also where the fabulous phoenix practised its art of resurrection and, since the bird was unknown in the West, a peacock took its place. It was believed that its flesh never decayed like the incorruptible Christian soul. A good example of this symbolism is its use by Hieronymous Bosch. In his *Ars Symbolica* he has blended every colour into the peacock's tail to express total unity.

PARTRIDGE

'For the king of Israel is come out
to seek a flea, as when one doth hunt
a partridge in the mountains'.
Book of Samuel I
The Bible

IN HEBREW THE partridge is called 'kore' which means 'to call or shout', and St Ambrose describes it as 'Satan tempting the multitudes with his voice'. No other bird has such a reputation for deceit and lasciviousness, and both Aristotle and Pliny agreed that the hen could be impregnated merely by the sound of the cock-partridge's call or scent. This is not surprising, as the love dance of the cock, hobbling on one foot with the other raised to ward off rivals, and the excited shrieking of the watching hens, is an orgiastic scene. The partridges become so absorbed in their ritual that even as man approaches to kill one of them, the rest will continue to dance, disregarding the death of their companion.

The island of Anaphe in the Aegean Sea was most famous for its partridges and the bird was sacred to the Cretan god, Talus. In Greek legend he was transformed into a partridge by the goddess Athene as he was being thrown to his death from the great height of her temple.

The partridge was a common bird in Palestine, and although much later it also became a symbol of the Church and truth, it is much maligned in the Scriptures. The caged partridge in the *Book of Ecclesiastes* is an allegory of a man who deceives his neighbours and is pleased at their disaster. The *Book of Jeremiah* says: 'As the partridge sitteth on eggs, and hatcheth them not; so he that getteth riches, and not by right, shall leave in the midst of his days, and at his end shall be a fool'. This last alleged habit of the partridge is certainly untrue.

CRANE

' Jane, Jane,
Tall as a crane,
The morning light creaks down again '.
An Aubade
Edith Sitwell

THE CRANE IS a symbol of vigilance, justice and the diligent man. An archaic bird, known to the early Chinese and the Egyptians as well as to the Hindus, it is mentioned in the Bible as ' knowing all seasons ', for its summers were passed in Europe and its winters among the ruins of the palaces of Pharaohs. The flight of the cranes is particularly beautiful and with its regular V-formations it is thought to have suggested the earliest hieroglyphics. Thoth, the Egyptian god of writing and the reformer of the calendar, was identified with an ibis, also a wading and sacred bird, similar enough to the crane for a connection to exist. To Ramakrishna, the crane was Kali's bird, and at the age of six he fainted with rapture at the sight of a flock flying low against the background of her temple.

The Greeks associated the crane with poets; partly because Apollo took the bird as his disguise when the gods had to flee from Greece, and partly because of the circumstances of Ibycus's death. Here the cranes were an instrument of justice, for when the sixth-century B.C. poet was attacked by a robber and lay dying, a flock of these birds was passing. Ibycus called out to them and they followed the murderer to a Corinthian theatre, hovering in the air until the guilty man was seized with fear and confessed his crime.

There is another legend of the vigilance of cranes. When at rest for the night, they form a circle around their leader and some are chosen to keep guard. The guardian cranes stand on one foot, the other half-raised clutching a stone. Should sleep threaten their watchfulness, the falling stone hitting the foot on the ground reminds them quickly of their grave responsibility.

WREN

'We'll shoot at a wren, says Robin to Bobbin,
We'll shoot at a wren, says Richard to Robin,
We'll shoot at a wren, says John all alone,
We'll shoot at a wren, says everyone'.
Nursery Rhyme
Anonymous

ITS GOLDEN crest a miniature crown, the wren was honoured by the Greeks and the Romans who called it 'little king of the birds.' The Druids also recognised its regal sign and an early legend tells how the first Christian envoys, angry at the respect shown to the wren, ordered it to be hunted and killed every Christmas. The superstitions concerning the killing of the bird at other times vary throughout Europe. In Brittany the 'fire of St Lawrence' afflicts any child that touches a young wren and lightning will strike the house of a killer of wrens. In parts of England, to rob a wren's nest will cause the thief to break a bone within the year and cows to give blood in their milk.

Wrenning Day still falls in December on the feast of St Stephen, and many local customs exist whereby the bird is cruelly stoned like the martyr saint or hunted to death. According to folklore, the tradition is seasonal rather than historical and it tells the tale of the turning year. A robin as a sign of the coming New Year, sets out to kill his father, the old King Wren whose reign must end. The murder is committed, the robin's breast is stained with red and the way is clear for the cycle to repeat itself.

CREATURES OF MUD & WATER

THE FISH is the main inhabitant of water, the primordial element of every mythology; a symbol of the unconscious and submerged nature of man. In the process of evolution, the element water united with the solid and receptive element earth, and mud was created to breed the reptile, crawling on its belly, covered with scales or horny plates. A half-caste of the universe, its home not on land nor in the sea; the family of the lizard, crab and snake changed into evil monsters and serpents to plague the imagination of man. Symbolically, the fish has always been more benign. It was a sign of fecundity among the Assyrians, the Chinese and the Babylonians, who first recognised it as the last sign of the zodiac and called it Kun or the 'tails'. The Chaldeans left their own particular mark on the fish by depicting it with the head of a swallow, meaning a herald of cyclic regeneration.

Although the fish was an important food throughout Egypt and the near East, the Bible, so precise about the names of birds and animals, classifies it only as clean or unclean. Even Jonah's whale is called simply a 'great fish', and of all the things that moved in the rivers and seas, those without fins or scales were forbidden as food. The curious showers of frogs and toads, mentioned in the *Book of Exodus*, must have also been common in ancient Greece; Aristotle refers to them as 'messengers of Jupiter'.

Astrologically, the age of Pisces began in 1 A.D., and with its appearance at the vernal equinox, the great phenomenon of Christianity came into existence. The fish is a sign of change, and a religion preaching selflessness and service to others was at the time a revolutionary idea. The five Greek letters forming the word 'ichthus' or fish, are also the initial letters of 'Jesus Christ God's Saviour', and this symbol was adopted by the early Christians. The disciples of Jesus became fishermen of souls, baptism by water a source of salvation, and the fish an emblem of spiritual renewal.

SNAKE

'The infernal serpent; he it was, whose guile,
Stirr'd up with envy and revenge, deceived
The mother of mankind'.

Paradise Lost
John Milton

FROM BABYLON to Greece, India and China to Europe, the eternal symbol of the snake crossed every path in the myth, culture and history of man. As the Egyptian Ra arose from the depth of the primeval water of Nun, the snake was the first to acclaim him god. In the shape of the great serpent Ophion, he entwined the divine limbs of the Greek Great Goddess and fathered the earth. An ally of monsters as well as the gods, he was the inspiration of the Nassenes and is still a source of ecstasy to the Holy Rollers of Kentucky.

The wisdom of the gods was the knowledge of the serpent; his sinuous form like the undulating waves of the sea which contain every secret and the mystery of life. Melampus, whose ears were licked by snakes, was the first mortal to be granted prophetic powers and to learn the language of the birds and insects. Garga, the father of Indian astronomy, owed his learning to a serpent. The god Quetzalcoatl, master of life, patron of the arts, and snake-bird, taught agriculture, metallurgy and gave the Aztecs maize and freedom from disease. Plutarch concluded that the serpent himself was a deity because 'it feeds upon its own body; even so all things spring from God, and will resolve into deity again'. The ouroboros, a symbol of the snake biting his own tail, was at the time adopted by the Gnostics, not only because it was a deity, but also because it represented the 'circle' or the 'wheel' of life, regeneration and eternity. The ability of the snake to shed its skin was confirmation of the belief in resurrection to the ancient sages and they thought that with its skin it also shed old age.

As a symbol of evil the coiled serpent of Midgard encircled the earth in the mythologies of the Norsemen. A serpent entwined the Tree of Life in the Garden of Paradise and first whispered the words of corruption to Eve. The woman succumbed and, like Hecate and Artemis who carry the snake in their hands or the grotesque Medusa whose tresses are made of reptilian coils, the shadow of sin endangered the spirit. The snake or the Devil lurks in the darkness to challenge the power of good; it is a symbol of seduction and the inherent evil in all the things of the world. But the snake coiled also around the caduceus of Mercury and the staff of Aesculapius, the god of medicine and healing. As good is balanced by evil,

so must health be offset by sickness, and the brass serpent of Moses was the healer of the wound caused by the serpent.

The coiled or triumphant serpent had to be vanquished; so the body of the snake nailed to a cross is found in the sixteenth century book of Abraham le Juif. There it is taken to mean the conquest of the spirit over the temptation of the woman and is also an undeciphered symbol of the union of the male and female principle in alchemy. In the Iliad, an eagle carrying a wounded snake in its claws appears to the Greeks. The crucified serpent is again symbolic of the triumph of the patriarchal Aryans, who have subdued the feminine and matriarchal tradition of Asia.

FROG

' Three monkeys tied to a clog,
  Two pudding ends would choke a dog,
   With a gaping wide-mouthed waddling frog '.
                    Nursery Rhyme
                    Anonymous

IN ANCIENT EGYPT the goddess Heket possessed the virtues, powers and body of a frog. Like all amphibious animals the frog is a symbol of fertility, and Heket who sprang from the wetness of Ra's mouth signified growth following decay. As the little frog of the Nile revived itself through its metamorphic cycle and announced the fertile flood, Heket revitalised the decomposing grain and assisted in the resurgence of the sun. Symbolic of resurrection, ornamental frog-gods were once placed on mummified Egyptian bodies, but the early Christians in an effort to stamp out every other religion, condemned the frog as a heretic and a devil.

Nevertheless, the cult of the frog has remained with us. In Africa the Bechuana warrior wears a frog charm around his neck to make himself as slippery to his enemies as the frog. A toad is still the god of the waters to the Orinoco Indian who, in time of drought, beats it with sticks knowing that it has the power to induce rainfall. And in some parts of Europe the Whitsun celebration still includes the killing of a frog, as rain is needed for a bountiful autumnal crop.

Folktales and legends mirror the earliest images, intuitions, experiences and thoughts of man. Almost universal among these is the allegory of a frog transformed into a prince. Since the animal is one of the most highly evolved cold-blooded creatures, Jung has suggested that the frog may easily have been the forerunner of man.

CROCODILE

' How doth the little crocodile
Improve his shining tail,
And pour the waters of the Nile
On every golden scale '.
Alice's Adventures in Wonderland
Lewis Carroll

WITH BRACELETS around his forelegs and golden rings piercing his ears, the old Petesuchos lived in a sacred lake close to the Temple of Crocodilopolis. An incarnation of the Egyptian god, Sebek, he was worshipped by the people of Faiyum and fed on cakes and honey-wine to assuage the powers of his evil fury. Like the serpent or the dragon he was a symbol of wisdom and universal knowledge to his devotees; a god-like creature, his eyes were covered with a transparent film through which he saw all, but was not seen himself. His vicious teeth, said to equal the number of days in the year, harmed nobody during the seven sacred days of Apis.

Plutarch explains that the crocodile was worshipped by the Egyptians for ' being the only animal without a tongue, like the Divine Logos, which standeth not in need of speech ', his power and virtue alone his greatest elo-quence. Inhabiting a realm somewhere between the earth and the water like the Demiurge which emerged to create the world, the crocodile also climbs to the muddy banks to lay its eggs. It is a symbol of the beginning and the powers of fecundity. Sometimes the crocodile stands for the plunge from the solid land of a ' material life ' into the ' mystic depths ' of spiritual experience, as it does in the twenty-first card of the Tarot.

Although respected by the native and killed only in retaliation, for centuries nobody has fed or worshipped Petesuchos. It is strange that today, on the shores of Lake Victoria in the heart of Africa, there lives an old crocodile called Lutembi. Every morning and evening for many generations, Lutembi has answered the call of the fishermen to receive an offering from their hands.

SNAIL

' Snail, snail,
Put out your horns,
I'll give you bread
And barley corns '.
Nursery Rhyme
Anonymous

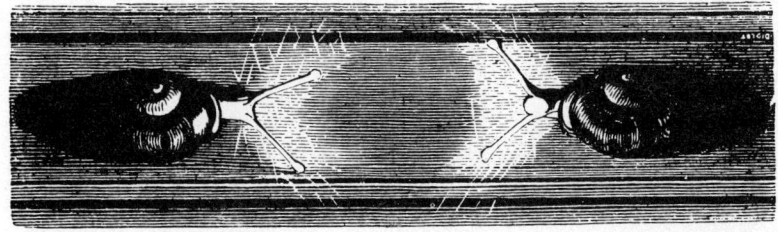

RHYMES TO invoke the appearance of a snail exist in almost every language of the world and contribute to folklore all over Europe, Russia and China. In Scotland and parts of England, the custom was to repeat such lines while holding a snail to a lighted candle and forcing it to leave its shell. If the creature obeyed the command, it was an omen of good weather. Although the snail is often a destroyer of crops, this tradition was meaningful, probably because the fine weather brought out a fruitful harvest along with the snail.

Christian thought connected the snail with the damp, muddy land it inhabited and with the idea that it feeds on slime. Forgetting that muddy waters are also a source of fertility, the snail was given the sinister symbolism of the sin of laziness and the decay of the spirit. Not so for the Aztecs, who honoured that which the Christians condemned. The Great Sea-Snail was for them the god of the moon and together with the pearl and the sea-shell, it was a sacred force of parturition, emanating from the waters, the moon and the woman.

No less significant is the spiral-shaped home of the snail. An ancient motif in all ornamental art, the spiral can be a simple curve or like a scroll it can turn in one direction or another. It is an image of the evolution of the universe, a circle of infinity and a sublime burden for the snail to carry on its back.

DOLPHIN

'Dies like the dolphin, whom each pang imbues
With a new colour as it gasps away,
The last still loveliest, till — 'tis gone,
and all is gray '.
Childe Harold's Pilgrimage
Lord Byron

ONE OF THE strongest and swiftest of fish, the dolphin is a symbol of salvation and the friend of man. As the waters grow calm after a storm the dolphins appear to the mariner, seeming to guide his boat; their colours brighter and more vivid when skimming the surface. In gratitude, Poseidon, the king of the sea, set the dolphin as a constellation in the sky. For had it not been for the messenger Delphinus, who pleaded the king's cause so eloquently, the beautiful Nereid, Amphitrite, would not have become Poseidon's wife.

In religious art, the dolphin is often portrayed bearing the souls of the dead across the seas to paradise. The fish became an emblem of the Church and sometimes of Christ Himself. But because the artists of the time had never seen a whale, the dolphin is painted as the 'big fish' swallowing Jonah, and like the whale it signifies the Resurrection. When intertwined with an anchor, its speed temporarily halted, the dolphin is a symbol of prudence and restraint.

Two adjoining dolphins, one pointing up and the other down, represent the cycle of life and, like a snake biting his own tail, stand for the continuity of time. This sign brought the dolphin into royal circles through the crest of Guy IX, the Count of Vienne. Under the Bourbons and the de Valois, the heir to the French throne held the title of 'Le Dauphin' perhaps as a symbol of continued monarchy, the saviour of his subjects and the French crown.

WHALE

'The hook was baited with a dragon's tail, —
And then on rock he stood to bob for whale'.
Britannia Triumphans
Sir William Davenant

ITS OPEN JAWS like the gaping gates of hell, its great bulk a legendary island deceiving the mariners of ancient days, the killer whale is still the most familiar and feared creature of the Pacific coast. It is a threat to the fishermen, capsizing their boats and stealing their haul; an evil monster but also a noble beast appearing in many Indian myths. The whale is the only mammal that evolved by leaving the earth and taking to the sea; although it is a close relative of the dolphin, there is little symbolic resemblance between them.

The whale has been hunted for many centuries, proving itself to be a fierce opponent. Whale-bone, oil, leather and ivory have always been valuable to man, and the giver of these gifts deserves some sanctity whether in Mada-gascar, Siberia or Greenland. Among the Eskimos there are many taboos concerning the killing of the white whale, for it is maintained that the soul stays within the carcass for four days. The villagers abstain from work and noise, and the use of sharp and iron tools is forbidden because the whale's spirit hovers invisibly and may be frightened or injured at that time.

The whale represents the allegorical sea-monster; its enormous shape is symbolic of the world and its mouth is the grave that received and concealed Jonah, only to disgorge him three days later. Thus the whale is also the sepulchre of the resurrected Christ and the universal image of the mother earth who receives in order to renew.

TURTLE

IN A HINDU myth the turtle stands indestructible, supporting an elephant which in turn supports the world; a symbol of universal order and perpetual existence. Of all the creatures that are at home both on the land and in the water, the turtle is the only one which essentially represents the fixed and material qualities of the earth. Its long life which stretches sometimes over many decades, its slowness of movement, even its obscurity, is symbolic of a terrestrial evolution.

As a cosmic symbol, the oriental image of a turtle is a circle on a square; the rounded shell standing for the heavens placed above the tangible world. But the square, the sign of great achievement in Egyptian hieroglyphics, best expresses the nature of the turtle. The sources of stability and order in the world are all related to the square, which is used as a base for construction and as a symbol of practical and rational thought. There are four seasons, four elements and four points of the compass. These are constant and ensure the natural equilibrium of life. If the turtle represents the square or the earth, and the earth is female in essence, the Biblical purification of women by turtles acquires a further and more complex symbolic meaning.

WORM

' A man may fish with the worm
that hath eat of a king, and eat
of the fish that hath fed of that worm '.
Hamlet
Shakespeare

THE WORM IS a symbol of death. Its name was once used for the serpents and snakes that fought with the Norse and Teutonic gods, and like these limbless creatures it crawls on the earth devouring life and breeding disaster. But the worm is no longer a monster, it is an abject and grovelling vermin, which in the form of the maggot devoured Herod ' because he gave not God the glory '. Literary and Biblical allusions to the worm connect it with death, vileness and contempt, so when David prayed in distress at his own insignificance, he cried: ' But I am a worm, and no man; a reproach of man, and despised of men '.

In Shakespeare's days there was a popular belief that little round worms bred in the idle fingers of the maid-servant, and an earthworm wrapped around a mixture of periwinkle and leeks was a potent love charm. But to William Blake, the invisible worm flew in the howling storm and destroyed the rose with his dark and secret love.

As a specific remedy against worms of the stomach, the herbalists prescribe wormwood. A plant symbolic of bitter experience and growing in the wastelands all over Europe, it is an ingredient in the making of absinthe. Wormwood inherited its name from an old legend which says that it sprang up in the track of the serpent as it slid along the ground when driven away from paradise.

INSECTS

TREATED WITH disdain as the most primitive member of the animal kingdom, the insect has, however, invaded mythology and legend as powerfully as any other creature. The strange complexity of its being has fired the imagination of man, who observed its habits and related them to his own ideas on existence. The nature of the insect varies from the parasitic louse to the aggressive wasp or ant and to the delicate and idling butterfly that is a symbol of joy and conjugal bliss in China. The world of the insect has followed its own pattern of evolution, sometimes superior to human life. Architects of their cities, co-operative members of a society, many insects have highly sophisticated means for the care of their young and for the protection of their groups. Among the colonies of ants, many supervise other insects for their living, some are mushroom farmers and others do nothing themselves, living off slave ants.

Since the insect feeds on living as well as dead matter, it is often a terrible threat to human life. Plagues of locusts and swarms of flies can level the forests of man, devour his crops and reduce him to despair. A single domestic fly can give birth to eight hundred thousand young flies in three months, and it is said that three flies can destroy the dead body of a horse as quickly as a lion. The power of the frail and weak lies in their number. So a multitude of insects is a symbol of degeneration and evil which in the past was averted only through the worship of Beelzebub and the Cyrenean Achor.

Born in one shape, the insect often dies in another. The emerald-winged scarab, the sacred beetle of ancient Egypt, bears no resemblance to the ugly, subterranean worm to which it owes its existence. Yet one was sanctified and symbolic of the migrating soul, and the other was a mass of knotted energy connected with death and decay. Little was known about the dramatic changes in the life of the insect until the Renaissance; even Aristotle, whose genius contributed much to the knowledge of animal history, had only a suspicion of the metamorphosis of insects. Since the psychological and spiritual urge of man is towards the transformation of his state, the life cycle of an insect is the perfect symbolic example of this aim. The paradox of death which permits birth can also change evil to good, hate into love and destruction into a creative force. The opposites can unite, fuse together for an instant and become inverted to answer this need. A symbol of such inversion is the cross of St Andrew, the letter X or, in the animal world, creatures that oppose each other like the wasp and the bee, the scorpion and the scarab.

BEE

'The pedigree of honey
Does not concern the bee;
A clover, any time, to him
Is aristocracy'.
Poems, Nature
Emily Dickinson

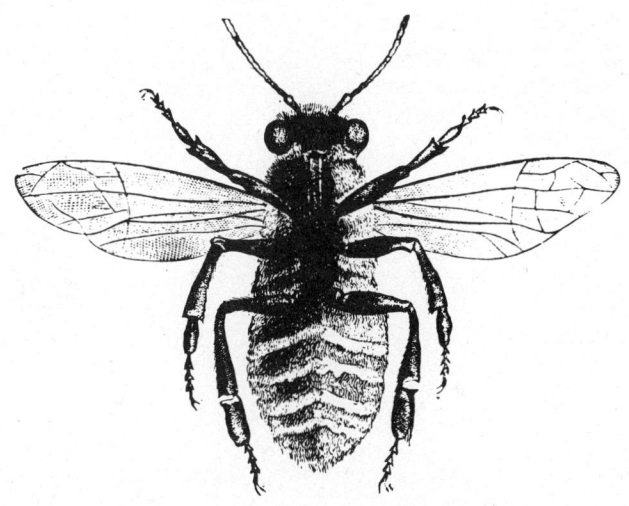

A ROYAL INSECT from the earliest history of Egypt, the bee is a symbol of industry, order and wealth. The beehive has always been an example of an ideally functioning society, reminiscent of the mythological Golden Age when man lived on honey that dripped from the trees. Old legends say that Jupiter was nourished by the bees, that the lyric poet, Pindar of Thebes, fed only on honey and that the sweet eloquence of Plato was a gift from a swarm of bees which alighted on his mouth when he lay in his cradle. According to the Orphic tradition, the bee had a deep spiritual significance. Human souls were thought to travel in swarms and, like swarms of bees leaving their hives touched with the goodness and sweetness of honey, they flew towards heaven, so that even Mohammed admitted the

bee to the Moslem paradise. In Christian symbolism St Ambrose was blessed with the 'honeyed words' of religious eloquence, and in his writing he compared the Church to a beehive, and a diligent Christian, working for the good of his hive, to the busy bee.

The city of Athens was once famous for its honey and the second great temple of Delphi was supposedly built by a swarm of bees; while the best known bee-keeper of Greek mythology was Butes who practised his craft on the Sicilian Mount Eryx. But Virgil tells us that the traditional honours for teaching the Arcadians new methods of bee-keeping were given to Aristaeus. When the bees in his hives sickened and died, his mother, the nymph Cyrene, told him to sacrifice four young bulls and four heifers and to leave their carcasses on an altar for nine days. In the stories of Samson and of Hercules, new swarms of young bees also emerged from the rotting flesh of animals and settled on nearby trees.

A special relationship has always existed between the bee and his master and in some parts of the country bees are known to be very sensitive to the fortunes of their keepers. Unless a black cloth is tied to the hives at times of mourning and a red one at times of joy and celebration, the insects do not thrive. Demonologists say that if a queen bee is swallowed by a witch it will help her to survive trial and torture without making a confession.

Just as the lily was connected with the Bourbons, so the bee was an emblem chosen by Napoleon. One hundred and fifty years before he was crowned as Emperor, the Tomb of Childeric revealed three hundred tiny golden bee models. He ordered that the bees should decorate his coronation gown and once more the bee became a symbol of monarchy, riches and order.

SCORPION

' The Mind, that broods o'er guilty woes,
Is like the Scorpion girt by fire; . . .
One sad and sole relief she knows,
The sting she nourish'd for her foes '.

The Giaour
Lord Byron

THE TREACHEROUS scorpion is an emblem of the hangman. Unlike the nurturing, honey-giving bee, the scorpion's poisonous sting is a threat of death and a symbol of the final ' fall ' of man. But on the inner walls of the sarcophagi, the Egyptian scorpion-goddess, Selket, was pictured with winged and extended arms as if to protect the mummified corpses from eternal death. Although merciless, the scorpion was still connected with the idea of regeneration. Biblical chastisement by scorpions (thonged whips tipped with metal spikes) expiated crime while legend claims that, within its body, the creature concealed the power to heal. In his Hudibras, Samuel Butler says:

' 'Tis true, a scorpion's oil is said
To cure the wounds the venom made,
And weapons dress'd with salves restore
And heal the hurts they gave before '.

Such oil was extracted from the flesh of a scorpion, used as medication and considered particularly good for kidney stones. Another belief was that if a scorpion was surrounded by fire it would sting itself to death with its own tail.

The scorpion is the eighth sign of the zodiac and was raised to the skies by Jupiter. This particular myth refers to the boasting of Orion whose vain claims that he could vanquish any animal on earth, were punished by the sting of a scorpion. But astrologically the scorpion is a water sign; resilient, passionate and intense, arising from the secret depths of chaos from which the world was originally formed.

SPIDER

' Much like a subtle spider which doth sit
In middle of her web, which spreadeth wide;
If aught do touch the utmost thread of it
She feels it instantly on every side '.
The Immortality of the Soul
Sir John Davies

IN THE CENTRE of the cobweb which is a symbol of human frailty and illusion, the spider sits awaiting its prey. Sometimes it is the Devil snaring a Christian soul but, more often, it represents the moon spinning only in the darkness of the night, an eternal weaver of the destiny of man. An American Indian myth sees the constellation of the Great Bear as seven brave men changed into stars and climbing to paradise by unrolling a spider's web. Symbolic of every creative action as well as a destroying force, the spider is an image of the alternating current of energy on which the very existence of the universe depends.

Like the malice of Satan, the venom of a spider was an evil curse of the old wives' tale. A witness at the murder trial of Sir Thomas Overbury in 1613 testified that he produced seven great spiders when asked to bring the strongest poison that he could find. And yet a common cure for jaundice was to swallow the live insect rolled in butter, and it was worn around the neck as a charm. Robert Burton, in his *Anatomy of Melancholy,* says: ' I first observed this amulet of a spider in a nut-shell lapped in silk, so applied for an ague by my mother. This methought was most absurd and ridiculous, I could see no warrant for it. Till at length, rambling amongst authors I found this very medicine in Dioscorides, approved by Matthiolus, repeated by Aldrovandus, in his chapter on spiders, in his book on insects, I began to have a better opinion of it '.

BEETLE

'O'er folded blooms
On swirls of musk,
The beetle booms adown the glooms
And bumps along the dusk'.
The Beetle
James Whitcomb Riley

THE BEETLE symbolises an eternal renewal of the life cycle in nature and owes this image to the Egyptian scarab or dung-beetle. For the Heliopolitans the scarab-faced god was Khepri, and the beetle sign was used for the word ' khope ' which meant ' to become '. On earth, the scarab beetle lays its egg and rolls it in dung or mud with its two hind legs which are long and crooked for this purpose. With extra-ordinary perseverence, like the legendary Sisyphus, it pushes its burden along until the size of the ball becomes larger than the beetle itself and a suitable place is found to abandon the now well protected egg. So in heaven the giant scarab, Khepri, rolls before him the incandescent globe of the sun at sun-rise and pushes it over the horizon when the day is set.

Because of its association with decomposing matter or dung, the beetle corresponds also to the stage of ' putrefaction ' in alchemy, a condition of decay and spiritual exhaustion from which new life arises. It is not surprising that the Egyptians venerated the scarab, mummified its body and immortalised its image on the monuments of Pharoahs and in their temples. Made of polished or glazed stone, set in precious metals and worn as an amulet or used as a seal, pendant or signet ring, the inscribed scarab concealed the secret of eternal life and was the sacred eye of the sun-god, Horus.

GRASSHOPPER

' The almond tree shall flourish, and the
grasshopper shall be a burden, and desire shall fail '.

Book of Ecclesiastes
The Bible

AN EMBLEM OF destruction, the grasshopper or the locust still travels in swarms through Palestine and Egypt ravaging every crop, tree and herb in sight. Pharaoh was cursed by a plague of locusts and it was the threat of the Lord for the disobedience of Israel. To St John the Divine, ' the shapes of the locusts were like unto horses prepared unto battle; and on their heads were as it were crowns like gold, and their faces were as the faces of men. And they had hair as the hair of women, and their teeth were as the teeth of lions. And they had breastplates of iron; and the sound of their wings was as the sound of chariots of many horses running to battle '.

Pharaoh's daughter used the magic of red thread and three locusts to seduce the mighty King Solomon. A golden locust was an emblem of the sun-god Apollo, chosen perhaps to warn against the scorching rays of the sun that bring drought and harm to all vegetation. In the reign of Queen Elizabeth the grasshopper appeared again. This time it was made of stone and decorated the original building of the Royal Exchange, perhaps to commemorate the crest of Sir Thomas Gresham, the founder. But it has stayed on the sign-boards of goldsmiths and bankers of London, possibly to avert financial disaster as much as to honour Sir Thomas.

ANT

' The ants are people not strong,
Yet they prepare their meat in the summer '.
Book of Proverbs
The Bible

IMMORTALISED in the *Book of Proverbs* and through Aesop's fables, the ant has become an example of thrift, perseverence and industry. ' Go to the ant, thou sluggard ', says the Bible, ' consider her ways and be wise '. This is the moral that Aesop conveys through his tale of the idling grasshopper. In parts of Morocco this idea is literally interpreted; the busy little ant is given to the listless patient to swallow in the hope that it will make him more active.

As a goddess of agriculture, Ceres, in particular, was concerned with the ant, whose actions and movements were a means of prophecy in the Roman temples. To act as a charm and to ward off evil, the ant and other insects were often preserved in the translucent amber which Francis Bacon called ' a more than royal tomb '. Since primitive societies have always thought that demons are as sensitive to pain as human beings, the Apalai Indian still subjects himself to the painful bite of the black ant so that his body and soul are purified. In a Hindu myth the ant symbolises the frail nature of existence and the pettiness of life, yet, in the words of Stephen Vincent Benet, ' the ant finds kingdoms in a foot of ground '.

FLY

' Dead flies cause ointment of the
apothecary to send forth a stinking
savour: so doth a little folly him that
is in reputation for wisdom and honour '.
Book of Ecclesiastes
The Bible

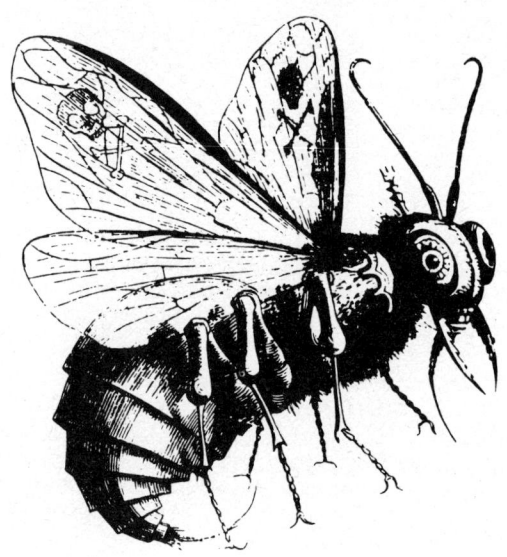

IT IS SAID that no fly was ever seen in Solomon's temple because, as the bearer of pestilence and disease, the fly was a symbol of evil and sin. The Romans made sacrifices to the fly in the temple of Hercules Victor, while the Greeks chose Zeus Apomyios as their protector against the insidious insect. A Mohammedan legend has it that all flies but the bee-fly shall perish, and the Christians in their early art showed the fly in the company of a goldfinch, the symbolic redeemer of diseased souls.

But the best known ' Lord of the Flies ' is Beelzebub. As Beelzebuth, he is one of the three supreme powers of evil in the *Grand Grimoire,* and when summoned by the magicians of the Middle Ages, he appeared as a gigantic fly. To the Jews at the time of Christ, his name was connected with the Philistine god of the city of Ekron, so he became the chief image of the false gods and the ' prince of the devils '. Whether Beelzebub means the ' lord who drives away flies ', or whether the priests of the god of Ekron used the fly for their auguries, is not known. The certain tradition of his evil prompts Milton when speaking of Satan to say:

' One next himself in power, and next in crime,
Long after known in Palestine, and named
Beelzebub '.

TREES & PLANTS

SINCE MAN has always searched for identity with the world around him, nature in the form of plant and tree life provided him with an image of his own existence. Unlike most animals, man's upright position closely resembles a shrub, the trunk of a tree or a stalk of corn. But above all, the annual cycle of growth and decay symbolises for him the mystery of death and resurrection; the fertility of his fields reflects a most powerful idea of a material, cosmic and spiritual regeneration. A forest in folklore and legend is symbolic of darkness and the unknown, the unconscious and the feminine. It is a place where vegetation thrives, threatening and uncontrolled and, in Druid mythology, it was a perfect partner in marriage to the vital and male emblem of the sun.

The worship of the tree is eternal and although certain species have been singled out to represent one deity or another, the symbol of immortality is common to them all. With its roots in the ground, its trunk a giant axis of the world and its branches stretching towards the sky, the tree symbolises the unity of the underworld, the earth and the heavens. As the oak was sacred to the Celts, the cedar to Osiris and the laurel to Apollo, so the vine bush inspired Bacchus and the fig tree brought enlightenment to the Buddha. The custom of planting trees on a grave began in China and the vitality of many evergreens was thought to give strength to the wandering spirit of the dead. There, the cherry, the bamboo and the pine often appeared together as the ' three friends ' who symbolised fertility and a long and happy life.

The tree as a symbolic axis of the universe has been traced to pre-Neolithic times and as such it has occupied the centre of the cosmos. It is the Yggdrasil of the Nordic myth, the Mesopotamian ' hom ' brought to the far East and to the West by the Arabs and the Byzantines, the Christian Cross of Redemption, and the inverted Tree of the Upanishads and the Zohar, growing downwards with its roots planted in heaven. The Biblical Tree of Life grew also in the Garden of Eden but it was from the Tree of Knowledge that Adam and Eve stole the apple and though gaining the wisdom of good and evil, they failed to become immortal. Perhaps the Tree of Life was hidden from them like the plant of immortality which Gilgamesh searched for at the bottom of the sea, for the path to eternal existence must be arduous.

Although a tree was not used as gallows until the Middle Ages, in Biblical times it still served as a witness to the punishment of crime, and the body of the condemned dead was hung on its branches for all to see. On the watery lowlands of Babylonia and the deserts of Palestine, the tree was rare and a gift of God to the Hebrews. The olive especially was the bearer of fruit and it was sacred because before the old tree dies, it grows new shoots to continue life. In gratitude to God, the law of Leviticus offered the first fruits to Him and forbade the eating of such fruit for four years. But because pagan tree worship was so popular in the Canaanite enemy hills where the ' asherah ' concealed the goddess of fertility, many leaders of Israel decried the cult and Isaiah prophesied: ' For they shall be ashamed of the oaks which ye have desired, and ye shall be cofounded for the gardens ye have chose. For ye shall be as an oak whose leaf fadeth, and as a garden that hath no water '.

LAUREL

' Cut is the branch that might have grown full straight,
And burned is Apollo's laurel bough,
That sometimes grew within this learned man '.
Doctor Faustus
Christopher Marlowe

THE EVERGREEN leaf of the laurel tree is a symbol of eternity, victory and triumph. In ancient Greece and Rome, the winner of a contest was crowned with a laurel wreath, which St Paul compared to the reward given to a good Christian: ' Know ye not that they which run in a race run all, but one receiveth the prize? So run that ye may obtain. Now they do it to obtain a corruptible crown; but we an incorruptible '. The laurel is also associated with chastity as it was once consecrated to the Vestal Virgins of Rome.

As a source of inspiration, the laurel was the tree of Apollo, the god of poetry, although he delegated this patronage chiefly to his retenue of Muses. His poets he rewarded with garlands of laurel, if they pleased and served him well.

The Pythia, Apollo's priestess at the temple of Delphi, chewed laurel leaves to induce a euphoric state for her prophecies, which were chanted in hexameter verse. The connection between poetry and the laurel is not only that the laurel is an emblem of immortality, but it is also a strong intoxicant. Eliphas Levi, in his works on the occult, recommends the burning of laurel juice, camphor and salt when preparing for magical rites; this induces a state of delirium in the magician. In the seventeenth century Robert Burton wrote: ' Laurel, by Heurnius, is put amongst the strong purgers of melancholy; it is hot and dry in the fourth degree. Pliny sets down fifteen berries in drink for a sufficient potion '.

YEW

' The bow was made in England,
Of true wood, of yew wood,
The wood of English bows '.
The Song of the Bow
Sir Arthur Conan Doyle

SACRED TO Hecate in ancient Greece and Rome, the yew is the tree of death and its branches were used as wreaths for the sacrificial bulls whose blood flowed to satisfy the thirsty ghosts that formed the retinue of the goddess. A native of Britain, it is a tree that matures slowly and lives to a great old age, and the Romans learned from the English that its hard, elastic wood made a perfect longbow; this enhanced the deadly image of the yew. As an evergreen the yew was often planted in churchyards, where it was said to spread its roots to the mouth of every corpse; but to grow it near a house was said to cause a family death. One of the oldest yew trees stands near Darley church in Derbyshire and is reputed to have been there for over two thousand years.

Traditionally the yew-berry is poisonous and the Celts combined it with ' helle-bore and devil's bit ' and applied it to their arrowheads. Shakespeare calls it the ' double fatal yew ' and the witch's cauldron in Macbeth contained a potion with some ' slips of yew, silver'd in the moon's eclipse '. But, according to Suetonius, the only remedy against the bite of a viper was the juice of the yew; this, in fact, is still widely used in homeopathic medications.

CYPRESS

' When I am dead, my dearest,
Sing no sad songs for me;
Plant thou no roses at my head,
Nor shady cypress tree '.
Song
Christina Rossetti

THE CYPRESS IS the tree of death and once its dark and evergreen foliage is cut down it never grows again. Dedicated to Pluto, the god of the infernal regions, the finest cypress wood was carved to make a Roman coffin and branches were thrown into the grave to speed the underworld passage of the soul before it reached the Elysian fields. Mentioned only once in the Bible, when Jacob is foretold the destruction of Babylon, the cypress is warned against as the wood from which ' graven images ' are made.

In Greek mythology Cyparissus was loved dearly by Apollo and the god changed him into a cypress when the young man's careless arrow killed his favourite stag. The tree was also sacred to Artemis who, like Apollo, was a deity of sudden death, and it grew in her honour at the holy grove in Marseilles when the city belonged to Greece. Lucan's account of Julius Caesar's conquest of Gaul especially mentions the ancient cypress, oak and alders which nobody dared to fell. But Marseilles was to become a fortress and the grove of trees was in the way, so Caesar had to use an axe himself before his soldiers were induced to carry out the work of desecration.

FERN

'I had
No medicine, sir, to go invisible
No fern-seed in my pocket'.
New Inn
Ben Jonson

A SYMBOL OF great sincerity and humility, the fern conceals its delicate charm in the shaded parts of wood and forest, unnoticed and forgotten. But twice a year, at Christmas and midsummer, when the sun pauses before returning on its course, the mythical fern flower blooms like shining gold or fire. In an old Germanic folk-tale, a hunter shoots his arrow at the midsummer sun, and the drops of blood which fall into his hands are changed into three glowing fern seeds. On those two mystic days, therefore, the forests of Europe and Russia are searched at midnight for the quickly fading fern flower; the seed that issues from the golden sun must also find the gold on earth. According to folklore, the finder of the bloom or seed need only throw it in the air for a hidden treasure to be revealed.

Other legends say that the flower is only seen by the good and honest searcher and when found, it will protect him from every evil force. But because it shows itself so seldom, it was once believed that the fern seed had the power to make its owner quite invisible. In the *Book of St Albans*, dating back to the fifteenth century, a recipe is found for making oneself as unseen as 'if one had partaken of fern seed'.

MYRTLE

'Know ye the land where the cypress and myrtle
Are emblems of deeds that are done in their clime;
Where the rage of the vulture, the love of the turtle,
Now melt into sorrow, now madden to crime'.

The Bride of Abydos
Lord Byron

ADMIRED FOR its white flowers and fragrant berries, the myrtle thrives best near the Mediterranean shore. It is the tree of Venus who courted her Adonis in the pleasant shades of a myrtle grove and its boughs were used to build the 'booths' at the Hebrew Feast of Tabernacles. In his call to the faithful, the prophet Isaiah gives the myrtle an image of joy by saying that: 'instead of the brier shall come up the myrtle trees', and 'all the trees of the field shall clap their hands'.

But the shade of the myrtle was once the shadow of the death of kings; its evergreen and curative leaves a symbol of renewal which the Greeks carried with them when they settled in new lands. Myrtilus was the son of Hermes and when bribed to loosen the chariot wheel of his master the King of Elis, he was drowned by the ungrateful Pelops who won the race and married the King's daughter. Hermes avenged the death of Myrtilus and laid a curse on Pelops and his house which suffered terrible tortures and crimes. The myrtle was also connected with the murdered Polydorus, the son of Priam. Virgil says that when Aeneas plucked the tree to decorate a sacrificial stone, the voice of Polydorus begged mercy from the ground and the myrtle dripped with blood.

CEDAR

THE MAJESTY and beauty of the cedar tree, specially that of the Lebanon cedar, is used by the prophet Ezekiel as a symbol of the Messiah and of his kingdom. Today an ancient colony of the trees, for the cedar grows very slowly, remains at the head of the deep valley of Qadisha near Bsherreh. The reddish bark is frosted with white and spans the thick girth of the trunks, as the flat evergreen branches spread out as wide as the tree is high.

The fumes of the sacred wood smoke inspired Hindu prophecies and in black magic the benevolent Jupiter, a planet of success, claims the sweet burning scent of cedar for his very own. A coarse-grained, strong and durable wood, the fragrant cedar takes fine polish and was used in making musical instruments, carvings and coffins. It was honoured by David and Solomon, ' and Hiram King of Tyre sent messengers to David, and cedar trees and carpenters and masons: and they built David an house '. But Solomon ' built also the house of the forest of Lebanon, . . . upon four rows of cedar pillars, with cedar beams upon the pillars . . . And the cedar of the house within was carved with knops and open flowers: all was cedar; there was no stone seen '.

A mountain of cedars appears also in the myth of Gilgamesh, and there he fought and conquered Khumbaba the Strong, whose dwelling place was among these stately trees. But the legend probably refers to the mountain of Amanus which lies between Syria and Asia Minor and where, on ascending the Euphrates, the early Babylonians found much needed cedar wood and stone.

OLIVE

'Incertainties now crown themselves assured,
And peace proclaims olives of endless age'.
Sonnet
Shakespeare

AN OLIVE BRANCH has always been regarded as an emblem of peace. A wreath of olive leaves was the highest distinction in ancient Athens and the coveted prize in Olympic games. According to legend, Athene and Poseidon competed for the possession of Attica in the days of King Cecrops. Poseidon's gift to the people of Athens was a horse, while Athene in her turn offered an olive tree which grew on the Acropolis. The dispute was settled in favour of Athene and she ruled in peaceful benevolence, while her tree gave wealth to her subjects and miraculously survived the invasion of Xerxes.

Moses called Palestine a 'land of oil', because there the olive grew profusely. A true Biblical tree, it is 'full of fatness' and was symbolic of God's care for the children of Israel. Jotham's parable in the *Book of Judges* tells that the trees wished to anoint their own king: 'And they said unto the olive tree, Reign thou over us. But the olive tree said unto them, Should I leave my fatness, wherewith by me they honour God and man, and go to be promoted over the trees'? Although the tree grows for many decades, peace is essential for the cultivation of the olive since it requires grafting and care to produce good fruit. In the story of the flood, a dove brought an olive leaf in his beak to signify to Noah that God had made his peace with man. Similarly, an olive branch and a dove are often used to signify that the soul of a dead man has passed away in the peace of God.

PALM

'No hammer fell, no ponderous axes rung,
Like some tall palm the mystic fabric sprung,
Majestic silence'!

Palestine
Reginald Heber

THE PALM TREE owes its name to the palm of the hand. Since it has no branches, it spreads fan-like from its crown, the leaves resembling fingers. As a symbol of prosperity in Biblical times, the palm was a 'goodly tree', growing in oases like Jericho, 'the city of palm trees'. There the palm yielded sugar, oil, tannin and juice for making arrak, while its leaves were used for thatching and to make baskets. The waving of palm leaves was an expression of joy and celebration among the Hebrews. This is mentioned in connection with the Feast of the Booths, and in St Matthew's account of the entry of Jesus into Jerusalem on Palm Sunday. For the Romans, the palm was a symbol of victory, and as such, it was later adopted by the Christians. The palm leaf was used to represent the triumph of a Roman gladiator, as well as the victory of Christ over death and sin.

An important symbol of fertility, the palm is a tree of life in the Babylonian garden of paradise. The legendary phoenix was also said to have been born and reborn in the palm tree. Because the tree grows best near water, with its head in the sun and its roots almost plunged into the sea, it is a symbol of birth; the sea representing the Universal Mother from whom all life emerged. In Sicily, palm leaves blessed on Palm Sunday were hung to produce rain and good harvests, while in other Catholic countries, the ashes of the consecrated palm were mixed into seeds sown at Easter.

POPLAR

ACCORDING TO a Christian legend, the white poplar or aspen, was the tree chosen for the making of the Cross. When it realised the purpose for which it was being cut down, its leaves started to tremble with fear and have continued to do so ever since. Its image as a tree of life is further emphasised, because the leaves of the aspen are dark on one side and silver on the other. This opposition of colours is symbolically related to the distinctive qualities of the sun and the moon, which rule the universe. In mythology the poplar was sacred to Hercules. When he emerged triumphant after slaying the giant Kakus in a cave on the Aventine hills, he picked a branch of the poplar and wound it round his head. But as he descended into Hades, the upper side of the poplar leaves was blackened with flames, while the underside became bleached with his sweat.

This legend probably served to justify the difference between the black poplar and the aspen. In pre-Hellenic Greece, the black poplar was the tree of heroes; it foreshadowed death and belonged to Mother Earth. It was also the tree from which shields were originally carved. But the aspen was a symbol of beauty and a tree of the Elysian Fields. The beautiful nymph Leuce was loved by Pluto, and he changed her into a white poplar after her death. The Heliads, sisters of Phaeton, also became aspens when they mourned their brother, after his fall from the chariot of the sun.

WILLOW

'Underneath the abject willow,
Lover, sulk no more'.
On This Island
W. H. Auden

THE WILLOW TREE or osier, belonged to Hecate, originally a moon goddess, who became the invincible queen of the underworld. She reigned over demons and presided over the dead, weaving her magic to torment the world. The witches also claimed the willow, particularly in Northern Europe, and their ancient name, 'wicker', is connected with the tree. The willow leaf worn in a hat refers to unrequited or rejected love, and it was probably once a secret charm against the jealousy of the goddess of the moon. Thriving best when growing close to water, which in turn is associated with the moon, the willow, according to some gypsies, is also a source of vital energy and fertility. It is particularly helpful in childbirth and cures the sick and the old. This magic is probably attributed to the tree because no matter how often its branches are cut down, the willow continues to grow and flourish.

An inspiration to the lovelorn poet, the weeping willow is a symbol of sorrow and sadness. Since the Babylonian captivity of the people of Israel, which lasted for over fifty years, the willow has been a symbol of mourning. A legend says that its branches drooped with pity at the fate of Israel, while a psalm records: 'By the rivers of Babylon, there we sat down, yea, we wept, when we remembered Zion. We hanged our harps upon the willows in the midst thereof'.

FLOWERS & FRUIT

ON THE transient nature of life, the prophet Isaiah says: 'And the glorious beauty, which is on the head of the fat valley, shall be a fading flower, and the hasty fruit before the summer; which when he that looketh upon it seeth, while it is yet in his hand he eateth it up'. As the fruit depends on the flower, its role is fleeting and its function only to produce the seed which is a symbol of hope and secret potential. Unlike the unrestrained and wild growth of the forests and plains, the fruits and flowers that grow in a garden are selected and enclosed. They are the treasures and mysteries of the forbidden gardens of folklore and mythology, and the objects of secret desire. In literature, as a symbol of fertility and sexuality, the fruit is much exploited. The fig with its many seeds is used as an image of sensuous temptation and the peach, grooved and round is the fruit of female mystery. But in the representational and ornate art of the Renaissance, Christian painters invented a symbol for every virtue and vice, and as the pear became an allusion to the love of Christ for mankind, so the plum was used as an emblem of fidelity and independence.

Ancient Greece produced many flowers which found their way into mythology as well as into the legendary rites of the Eleusinian mysteries in honour of Demeter and her daughter Kore. The vanity of Narcissus caused him to be turned into the purple and white flower, and the love of Apollo for his dead companion Hyacinthus led to a revival of the memory of his fate with every returning spring. Both the Greeks and the Romans celebrated their festivals by wearing crowns of flowers and, like the Egyptians who brought skeletons to their banquets as reminders that the enjoyments of life are brief, they strewed flowers over the bodies of their dead, more in analogy than in offering.

The shape of a flower gives it a symbol of the 'centre' and for the alchemist who called the meteorite a 'celestial flower', it was also an image of the work of the sun. The lotus flower which grows abundantly in Egypt was the glory of the ancient Nile garden. It provided the design for the famous Fifth Dynasty lotus-column capitals which eight hundred years later became the centres of the Greek Ionic cities. The colour of flowers is no less significant. Whether the meaning of certain colours became constant through centuries-old associations, or whether they have an innate force of their own is disputable in the occult world. But flowers of orange or yellow have always corresponded to the sun, just as red, the colour of blood, passion and love is the traditional hue of the rose or the poppy. Related to the sky and to water and probably an allusion to the 'mystic centre' of both, is the flower of blue which stands for the legendary symbol of the impossible.

FIG

THE FIG TREE stands leafless through the winter but the first fruit buds appear in February or in March. Many are blown to the ground but those that mature are prized for their flavour and are the ' early figs ' which the Romans offered to Mercury. In spite of this, most proverbs consider the fruit of little value and it is a symbol of lust and ingratitude.

Unless it is tended by man the fig rarely produces its edible, many-seeded fruit. In Greece and Asia Minor the cultivated fig is sometimes fertilised by hanging on it strings of the small wild fruit. To stimulate this union, sexually suggestive ceremonial rites are performed by men and women. After the Fall of man, Adam and Eve ' sewed fig leaves together and made themselves aprons '; in the same way, the leaf was used on the naked statues and paintings of Victorian times when modesty was much in fashion.

There is a parasitic species of the fig which strangles its host with many aerial roots and this fact, together with the story of Judas who hanged himself on a fig tree, gives the fruit an accursed and ungrateful image. In memory of the withered tree, figs were eaten on Palm Sunday which used to be known as Fig Sunday. According to the gospel of St Mark, once when Jesus was hungry, he saw a fig tree but drawing near he saw that it had only leaves, ' for the time of the fruit was not yet '. And Jesus said unto it: ' No man shall eat fruit of thee hereafter for ever '. The next day the fig tree was dried up from the roots.

POPPY

' Drows'd with the fume of poppies, while thy hook
Spares the next swath and all its twined flowers '.

To Autumn
John Keats

AS THE NETTLE is the sting of death so the red poppy is a symbol of blood and the sleep of death. In the art of the Renaissance it alludes to the Passion of Christ and it appears on the Tarot card of the Day of Judgement when the dead are awakened from their long sleep by the trumpet of an angel. On Remembrance Day, the flower recalls the poppy fields in Flanders where death claimed many thousands of lives.

Because the fruit of the poppy is round and contains many black seeds it is sometimes a symbol of fertility. But it also signifies ignorance and indifference because its extract is opium, a powerful narcotic with a bitter taste and a heavy odour, which induces stupor and dulls the mind. In sorcery and witchcraft, most substances recommended for burning give off fumes causing comas, hallucinations or delirium. One formula for summoning the Devil is to burn hemlock, coriander, henbane and poppy; this mixture is also known to cause convulsions and even temporary insanity. Love charms are usually made of aphrodisiac herbs which are ground to powder and put into the food of the lady desired; but the poppy does not induce desire and its magic works only by drugging the victim into helplessness.

Poppy red is also the colour of extravagance, pomp and wealth, and the brilliant hue of the flower may have prompted Gilbert and Sullivan in the comic opera, *Patience*, to say: ' Though the Philistines may jostle, you will rank as an apostle in the high aesthetic band; If you walk down Piccadilly with a poppy or a lily in your mediaeval hand '.

APPLE

' And pluck till time and times are done
The silver apples of the moon,
The golden apples of the sun '.
The Song of Wandering Aengus
W. B. Yeats

WHETHER A SYMBOL of dispute, love or desire, the apple is woven into many legends and mythologies of the past. As the golden fruit of the ancients it was probably the apricot or the quince, for the true apple was unknown, although scholars have claimed that it grew wild in Solomon's time. In Latin, ' malum ' means ' an apple ', as well as ' evil ', and the Tree of Knowledge in the Garden of Eden was traditionally an apple tree, though the Bible never names the forbidden fruit. The importance of the legendary apple lies in its round and symmetrical shape, suggesting a circle or a sphere which are symbolic of immortality and a wholeness enclosing the material and spiritual values of man. The golden apples guarded by the goddes Idun were tasted by the gods whenever they wished to renew their youth, but the lovely apples of Sodom which grew on the shores of the Dead Sea brought disappointment and disillusion and were ' all ashes to the taste '.

The paradox of good and evil runs through every theme about the fruit. The Talmud says the apple is important to good health, thus emphasising its meaning of immortality, and in the tale of the Arabian nights, Prince Ahmed's apple cures all ills. Yet the apple offered to Snow White is poisoned and sends her into an oblivious sleep. The *Song of Solomon* says: ' As the apple tree among the trees of the wood, so is my beloved among the sons. I sat down under his shadow with great delight, and his fruit was sweet to my taste '.

This allusion to Christ makes the apple symbolic of goodness and the eternal life. If

Christ is the new Adam, the redeemer of sin, so in the hand of the Virgin Mary the apple is a symbol of salvation but in those of Eve it is a symbol of evil and temptation.

In the Celtic myth of King Curoi's soul which was hidden in an apple, which lay in the stomach of a salmon that appeared only once every seven years, Queen Blathnat took the hero Cuchulain as her lover. She revealed to him the King's secret, and they conspired to find the fruit. When at last the sword of Cuchulain severed the apple in half, all became darkness as the centre showed a five-pointed star, a symbol of immortality and the mystic sign of a divine power that man holds over the universe and evil.

POMEGRANATE

'Pomegranates like bright green stone,
And barbed, barbed with a crown.
Oh, crown of spiked green metal
Actually growing'!
Pomegranate
D. H. Lawrence

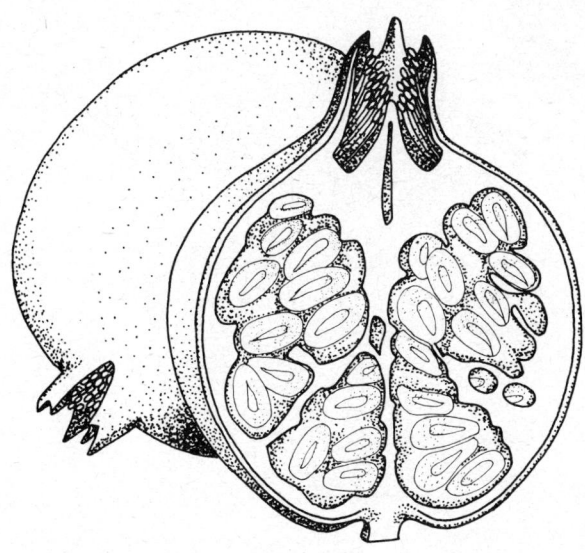

A SYMBOL OF fertility and unity, its round-ness filled with many succulent seeds, the pomegranate is a favourite of the Middle East. In Greek mythology, it belonged to Persephone who was abducted to the infernal regions of Hades and whose periodic return to the earth in springtime became symbolic of the fruit. Attis was to the Phrygians what Adonis was in Syria, and having been conceived by his mother Nana through the eating of a pome-granate seed, the idea of immortality and resurrection further enhanced the meaning of the fruit. The Egyptian Sekhmet, a savage lioness of war, was also associated with the pomegranate. When Ra saw her in the battle-field slaughtering every man, he despaired for the human race and filled seven thousand jugs with a magic potion made up of pomegranate juice. Mistaking the red liquid for blood, Sekh-met became too drunk to continue her warfare and mankind was saved.

The Biblical pomegranate was the only fruit allowed to be brought into the Holy of Holies and it decorated the robes of the High Priest while in the Jerusalem Temple built by Solo-mon, 'the pomegranates were two hundred in rows round about upon the other chapiter'. Although in the European Jewish tradition the Chanukah candlestick is surmounted by the Star of David, the place was originally occu-pied by the pomegranate as a symbol of rain and the many children or 'seeds' of Israel. It was also explained that the pomegranate was the only fruit uncorruptible by worms.

LILY

' Have you seen but a bright lily grow,
Before rude hands have touched it?
Have you marked but the fall o' the snow
Before the soil hath smutched it '?
Her Triumph
Ben Jonson

THE CHASTE AND innocent lily is the flower of the Virgin Mary and it is the symbol of her purity. One legend says that the lily sprang from the tears of Eve as she left the garden of Eden, full of remorse; but it is also an attribute of St Clare, St Dominic and St Francis in honour of their chastity. The Annunciation, a subject much painted during the Renaissance, is particularly associated with the lily, as the archangel Gabriel is usually pictured holding the flower or it is shown standing in a vase. The translucent glass of the vase is another symbol of pristine virtue and any receptacle alludes to the earthly and feminine idea of birth.

Many objects of art excavated in Egypt are decorated with the lily motif. It appeared on the coins of the Maccabean family who won religious and political independence from the Jews, and ruled from 166 to 37 B.C. But its heraldic interpretation, or the fleur-de-lis, dates back to the Middle Ages when the emblem of King Clovis was miraculously changed from three toads into a standard of three lilies in a field of azure blue. He called this new banner the oriflamme and it became a symbol of the French royalty and of religious illumination.

ANEMONE

'To me the meanest flower that blows can give
Thoughts that do often lie too deep for tears'.
Ode, Intimations of Immortality
William Wordsworth

WHEN A WILD bear killed Adonis, Venus lamented her lost love and in her sadness changed the blood from his wounded side into a red flower. Since the wind blows its delicate blossoms quickly away, the anemone is as short-lived as the young and beautiful hero to whom it owes its creation. It is a symbol of sorrow and death and the Arabs still call the anemone the 'wounds of Naaman', or 'darling', which was their name for Adonis. Mourned in the great Phoenician sanctuary at Byblos, the blood of Adonis was said to flow in the river each Easter and the women who first grieved his death, celebrated and rejoiced at the sight of this resurrection. Today, by the village of Jebeil near Beirut, the red earth washed down from the mountains by rain in springtime, still tinges the water a blood-red hue and the banks are briefly covered with the anemone in bloom.

In the early days of the Christian Church the triple leaf of the anemone symbolised the Holy Trinity. It was also said that the flowers sprang up on Calvary after the death of Christ. In her great sorrow at the crucifixion of Christ, the Virgin Mary, like the mourning Venus, was often depicted with a red anemone, the flower of suffering and pain.

BEAN

' And this is good old Boston,
The home of the bean and the cod,
Where the Lowells talk to the Cabots,
And the Cabots talk only to God '.
Toast proposed at Harvard dinner. 1910
J. C. Bossidy

THE EATING OF the bean was forbidden in ancient Greece and Rome since the plant was strongly connected with spirits and ghosts. According to mythology the bean was sacred to the goddess Demeter, who gave the Arcadians permission to plant every pulse and grain except for the bean. Since the plant grows spirally, it was associated with the resurrection, and by entering the bean footloose spirits contrived to be reborn as humans. Pythagoras forbade his disciples the use of beans. According to one interpretation, this meant abstaining from political action, since elections were then held by casting beans into a helmet. Others thought that, as he believed in the transmigration of the soul, the bean was not to be used as food. Nevertheless, two centuries later, the followers of Plato still abstained from the bean, this time on the rational grounds that it caused flatulence.

In the first century A.D., the Roman naturalist Pliny, records that the soul of the dead lives on in the bean, and that the best charm against ghosts and witches is to throw a bean at the spectre, giving it a chance to be reborn. The Romans were particularly troubled by the Lemures, who were the mischievous spirits of the dead, returning to torment the living. To drive them away, the father of the family would rise in the middle of the night, snap his fingers and wash his hands three times. Then he would fill his mouth with black beans and spit them behind him, saying: ' I throw away these beans and with them I redeem myself and mine '. The ninth, eleventh and thirteenth of May celebrated the exorcism of these ghosts.

126

But the myth of the bean did not die out with the Romans. The Scottish poet, Alexander Montgomerie, who was a laureate of the Scottish court in 1577, claimed that witches rode to their sabbath on a bean stalk. The bean was also once honoured with a feast on Twelfth Night. The king of the bean, or the person who had the good fortune to find a bean in a slice of cake, presided over ritual magic and invocations of good weather and crops. Today, the story of Jack and the Beanstalk is a popular fairytale. The bean for which Jack exchanges his cow, miraculously grows to reach the sky. There at the top of the beanstalk, in the shape of an ogre, lives a malevolant being, as evil as ever.

ROSE

'The red rose whispers of passion
And the white rose breathes of love;
O, the red rose is a falcon,
And the white rose is a dove'.
A White Rose
John Boyle O'Reilly

THE FLOWER OF Venus, a symbol of joy, victory and perfection, the single rose, like the mandala, stands for the mystic centre. In the language of flowers a wreath of roses means beauty and virtue rewarded; the faded rose is a reminder that beauty is fleeting; and the Dog rose, with thorns large and sharp, signifies pleasure and pain. The Virgin Mary is some-times called the 'rose without thorn' as the Christian Church claims that she was born unblemished by original sin. As a symbol of achievement, however, the golden rose belongs to the Pope. An ornament made of gold, the rose is filled with musk and balsam and, according to an ancient custom, is a reward for services to the Catholic Church. The last person to receive it with the papal blessing, was the Grand Duchess of Luxembourg in 1956. But the most significant of all is the red

and white rose. The two colours in ancient alchemy affirmed the conjunction of opposites; since red is the symbol of passion and white of purity, the curious alchemical red and white rose, symbolised a union of fire and water. This union was an ideal state of being, and the *Song of Solomon* praised the perfection of Christ by saying: 'My beloved is white and ruddy, and the chiefest among ten thousand'.

When a host in ancient Rome or Greece hung a rose above the table, his guests knew that every word spoken was to remain secret. Later roses were sculpted on the ceilings of council chambers, banquet rooms and con-fessionals as a symbol of discretion. The exact origin of the term 'sub rosa' is obscure, but there is a myth that Cupid once offered a rose to the god of silence, Harpokrates, bribing him not to disclose the amours of Venus.

ARTIFACTS

AN ARTIFACT is the creation of man, whether it is a house to give him shelter, a weapon to protect him from the enemy, or a bowl to contain his food. Man had to adapt himself to the world around him, and a sense of physical and spiritual order was necessary for his survival so he related anything that he created to this basic need. With the passage of time, the origin and the symbolic meaning of an object familiar in very day life has been lost, hidden or disguised. But the shape, function and character of anything made through human effort implies more than its obvious and conventional end, whether it has been shaped for the use, or for the pleasure of its maker.

To the early man meteorites and aerolites falling from the sky were associated with celestial power and deity, and because all iron first used by man was of meteoric origin, anything made of this metal had a sacred meaning. An iron knife has remained a protective weapon against evil spirits and demons, as not only does it serve to kill but it carries with it the blessing of the gods. An object such as a basket, symbolic of a more important container like the womb or the maternal body, is often linked in mythology with water, the primeval source of creation. Thus Semele, while she was bearing Bacchus, was placed in a basket and thrown into a river, and Moses in his bullrush cradle was floated among the reeds of the Nile. Utensils in particular seem to possess a certain mystic force which intensifies their symbolic value. But less complex objects simply represent a masculine or feminine motive; the anvil which is a passive emblem of the earth is acted upon by the hammer, simulating the power of fecundity. Some objects acquire their symbolism by association and these are the symbols of many saints, martyrs, gods or monsters belonging to legend. So the comb is an attribute of the siren as well as St Blaise who was tortured to death by combs of iron.

In art the Surrealist and Dada movements have attempted to point out the early and symbolic aspects of some objects, by stripping them of their conventional meaning and their daily use. A drinking cup becomes a chalice, a sacrificial vessel, or even a primitive drum. Max Ernst used the fan as a cosmic image to represent the world in a state of constant transformation and motion. Although it is an ancient Chinese emblem related to wind and air which revived the spirits of the dead, the Western fan is made to fold and like the moon affects the tides and the imagination. It can grow from a sliver to the fullness of a circle and is a symbol of change. The bracelet and the ring with their obvious implication of the closed circle, are both symbols of wholeness, continuity and an eternally repeated cycle of life. A popular image of marriage and love is the heart pierced with an arrow, and in primitive religions it signified a sacred union between heaven and earth.

The loss of an object is connected with sorrow and grief. In mythology and legend it is to lose oneself, or an eternal aspect of one's soul, the absence of which leads to a state similar to death. Although the loss can be blamed on chance or circumstance the real reason for such a death is to forget or to depart from the origin of one's being. The theme of the Quest is a significant journey to find the lost object which is sometimes symbolically expressed as the Golden Fleece or the Great Treasure, and the concept of the search and the subsequent rediscovery or reunion is also an analogy of death and the resurrection of man.

BELL

'Hear the loud alarum bells —
Brazen bells!
What a tale of terror, now, their
turbulency tells'!
The Bells
Edgar Allan Poe

SHAPED LIKE the heavenly vault, suspended between earth and the sky, the bell is a symbol of a mystic and protective power. It was eagerly adopted by Christianity and first installed in a church in Capania by the bishop of Nola, in the fourth century A.D. Although the *Book of Exodus* speaks of bells being used as tinkling ornaments on the robes of Jewish priests, there is little evidence of the bell before the Christian era. Instruments which called the Romans to public baths and processions were probably cymbals or resonant pieces of metal, like the timbrels used in the worship of Cybele, or the Egyptian sistrum, resembling a rattle. Tolling for death, danger or joy, bells have summoned soldiers to arms and Christians to church. Many a bloody chapter in history has been rung in and out by bells. On St Bartho-

lomew's day in 1572, they ushered in the massacre of the Huguenots in France; while the bells of Chester rang a happy peal, alternated with one deep toll, to announce the victory of Trafalgar and the news of Nelson's death.

Many old customs and beliefs are connected with the religious use of bells. The Japanese thought that souls of people approaching death, went to the temple and rapped or rang the 'spirit' bell, to announce their own departure to the priest. The Passing Bell used to be rung for the dying, but now it is only heard after death has taken place. Burial Peals, once common during funerals and sounded to frighten away the evil spirits from the soul of the departed, were finally banned in Puritan times, although strong superstition has kept them alive in other forms.

The belief that bells have the power to disperse and terrify bad spirits seems to have prevailed everywhere. Among some African tribes, bells have been worn as amulets, while in the presence of the sick they were tinkled to prevent demons from entering the weakened body. The bell is also an attribute of St Anthony Abbot, who in Renaissance art was pictured carrying a bell to symbolise his gift for exorcism. In the sixth century, when Justin II was trying to make peace with the Turks, his ambassadors were met by Turkish shamans with ringing bells and jangling tambourines. This was not a way of greeting, but an effort to frighten away the evil spirits that the strangers might have brought with them. As well as driving away the Devil, a consecrated bell had the power to extinguish fires, and to disperse storms and pestilence. As late as 1852, the Bishop of Malta ordered the church bells to be rung to ' lay a gale of wind '.

CROWN

WREATHS OF leaves or flowers were the first crowns worn by gods to mark their distinction. Later, the crown became a sign of royalty and it still retained some of the lofty symbolism of a tree. Placed above the head, like the topmost branches of a tree, the crown stands for the spiritual elevation of man, as well as his achievement on earth. In the republic of Rome, various crowns had different meanings and were rewards for bravery. The ' camp crown ' made of gold and decorated with palisades, was given to the first soldier to enter the fortress of the enemy. Oak leaves surrounded the ' civic crown ' received for slaying a foe and saving the life of a Roman citizen. The 'Iron Crown of Lombardy' is perhaps the oldest in Europe, and it owes its name to an iron fillet which is said to have been wrought out of a nail from the cross of Jesus. Charlemagne was crowned with it in 774 A.D. and Napoleon placed it on his own head in 1805; it was later returned to Italy and placed in the cathedral at Monza.

To the alchemist, the secret of making gold was a mark of divine favour. The conversion of base metals into gold, involved spiritual evolution in the alchemist himself, and reaching this goal was symbolised by the radiant crown of eternal life. Ancient magical texts represent these base metals as bareheaded slaves, bowing to gold, or their king and master. Later, they are shown upright and with crowns on their own heads, the process of transmutation having been completed.

HORN

'Have sight of Proteus rising from the sea;
Or hear old Triton blow his wreathed horn'.
The World Is Too Much With Us
William Wordsworth

WHETHER THEY appear on the Dionysian bull, the Devil's goat or the head of Moses, the horns of pre-historic times and the Middle Ages are symbolic of great power and strength. An ancient horned god was Cernunnos, and his cult was widespread, being found in the fourth century B.C. rock engravings in Italy, in Roman and Celtic sculptures, and carved into sandstone blocks in Ireland. Although little is known about him, his stag-like antlers possibly represented the cycle of fertility, and he was also associated with the serpent and the underworld, like the Devil. Horns came to mean an evil force, probably through a process of inversion, particularly in the occult world. Possibly they were also confused with the ox symbol; that of castration and sacrifice. An early evil sign was that of a hand with three

middle fingers closed and the two others extended, like horns on a head. Because two is the first number to break away from the unity, or the One of God, it is sacred to Satan. The three hidden fingers deny the Holy Trinity.

The horn as a sacred symbol of glory, victory and power, adorned battle helmets and hides of ancient warriors. For the Egyptians, the sign of the horn meant 'that above the head', and implied sanctity, as well as 'pushing ahead', like the battering-ram to clear the way. In astrology, Aries the ram symbolically performs this function when he ushers in the renewed cycle of the zodiacal year. Ancient Hebrew altars were decorated with horns and, although their origin is not known, they may have been the hooks which held the sacrificial animal. Smeared with the blood of slaughtered victims, these horns were holy and gave sanctuary to anyone who touched them. The *Book of Kings* relates how Adonijah, son of David, attempted to usurp his brother's throne, and 'feared because of Solomon, and arose, and went, and caught hold on the horns of the altar'.

A single and a hollow horn is the cornucopia, a mystical and feminine receptacle of goodness and plenty. Perhaps the fabled unicorn contributed to its bountiful powers; or the horn of a rhinoceros, which, carved into a cup in China, is an emblem of prosperity and strength. In Biblical times, flasks of hollowed horn contained anointing oils and healing mixtures; while the shophar which called the Hebrews to worship, is one of the oldest musical instruments. This horn of a ram, made flat and straightened with heat, perhaps commemorated the ancient ram once sacrificed by Abraham.

KEY

' The Pilot of the Galilean lake;
Two massy keys he bore of metals twain
(The golden opes, the iron shuts amain) '.
Lycidas
John Milton

A KEY IS A symbol of the unknown, which is revealed only on death or to the chosen few. Its meaning probably originates from the early Egyptian ' ankh ' sign, represented by the ansate cross, which stood for eternal life. Looped at the top and resembling a key, this cross was often shown being held by Egyptian gods in their ceremonies over the dead. The Christians adopted the image, and for them it became the key of St Peter, who opens the gates of heaven that lead to immortality. The insignia of the Pope, the successor of Peter, consists of two crossed keys made of silver and gold, and is an emblem of his supreme ecclesiastical authority. A key with a dove is often found in Romanesque art and this symbol again represents the spirit opening the gates of paradise.

In folklore or legend, a key is symbolic of some secret knowledge. After a long search, the finding of a key is the first step towards this discovery of the treasure, or spiritual truth. The progressive stages of such a quest are often symbolised by three doors which must be opened with keys of silver, gold or diamond. The two keys of precious metals represent understanding and wisdom, while the diamond one stands for the light and brilliance associated with the mystic centre. A key, like the knife, was also a charm against disease and demonical possession, since both these objects were originally made of iron, the metal of the gods. Clidomancy, one form of divination, was practised by placing a key on the Fiftieth Psalm and binding the Bible tightly with a virgin's garter. When the holy book was then suspended from a nail, it was believed to turn and twist when the thief's name was mentioned.

LADDER

' But we build the ladder by which we rise
From the lowly earth to the vaulted skies,
And we mount to its summit round by round '.
Gradatim
Josiah Gilbert Holland

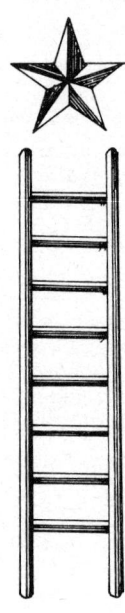

A LEGEND OF the golden age, when gods and mortals mingled in peace and harmony, exists in mythologies of every place and time. Only a ladder, a mountain or a tree, separated the earth from heaven before man offended his god. This original sin created a great rift between the two, and man's desire to return to a godly state is symbolised by a ladder. To climb it is to reach paradise; to descend it below the surface of the earth is to enter the infernal regions. According to the Koran, Mohammed saw a ladder which ' the just and the good climbed up to reach god '; while the Bible says of the vision of Jacob; ' And he dreamed, and behold a ladder set up on the earth, and the top of it reached to heaven: and behold the angels of God ascending and descending on it '. An image of opening the way from one world into another, or of breaking through the different levels of existence, the ladder is a symbol relating the passive state of the earth to the virtue of heaven, or the sin of hell.

To the ancient Egyptians, whose tombs revealed many amulets engraved with a ladder, the soul had to ascend nine symbolic rungs to reach the great Osiris. These steps represented the nine deities, who together with Osiris, made up the sacred number of ten; a numerical symbol of completing the cycle and a return to unity. The *Egyptian Book of the Dead* says: ' the gods make him a ladder, so that, by making use of it, he may go up to heaven '. The custom of a funerary ladder to aid the resurrection of the spirit, has survived until today and it is used among primitive Asian tribes.

An initiate into the mysteries of the Mithraic cult, the only serious rival to Christianity in Roman times, climbed seven mystic steps to become one with his God of light. Each rung of the ceremonial ladder was made of a different metal belonging to a corresponding planet, the seventh of which was the sun, whose metal was gold. As the ladder was climbed, the initiate passed through the seven heavens, just as one attained the ultimate heaven by ascending the seven stages of the Babylonian ziggurat, or as one travelled through the cosmic regions by scaling the terraces of the Buddhist Temple. In the Middle Ages, the idea of a gradual progress towards a state of perfection was also adopted by the alchemists, and was identified with the various phases in the making of the Philosopher's Stone. The ladder, as a symbol of ascension, was then frequently surmounted by a cross, a figure of an angel, or a star; all emblems of God.

SHELL

' Gather a shell from the strown beach
And listen at its lips: they sigh
The same desire and mystery,
The echo of the whole sea's speech '.
The Sea Limits
Dante Gabriel Rossetti

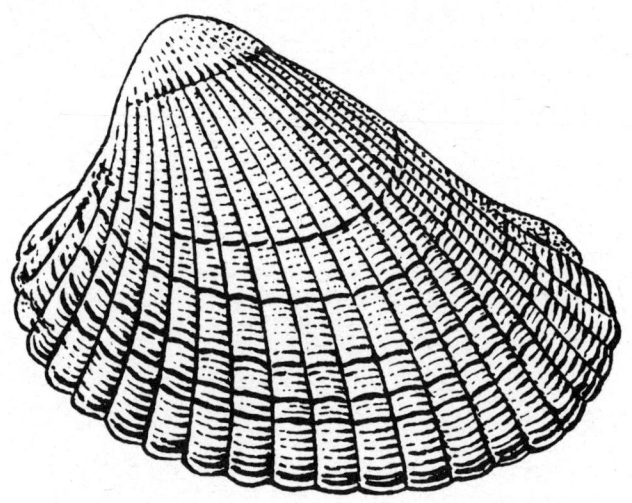

LONG BEFORE Aphrodite arose from her scallop shell, or the Tritons played among the waves, noisily blowing a conch, the shell was a mystic symbol of regeneration. The Red Sea offered it up to the early Egyptians, who made shell necklaces, bracelets and amulets to defend their women against sterility and misfortune. The sacred shell motif was inscribed on many tombs of pre-dynastic Egypt and was an emblem of hope and resurrection. Because its home is the primeval ocean and the shell is female in form, it has, like the pearl and the oyster, a magical force to aid parturition. The cult of the shell seems to have existed everywhere since prehistoric times. One of the symbols of Vishnu, the conch was used as a trumpet to announce the Hindu marriage. On another continent, it played an important role in the Aztec initiation rites and was a supreme symbol of spiritual rebirth. To ensure resurrection, an ancient Japanese custom was to anoint the body with a powdered sea shell; while in China justice was administered in the presence of a conch. A cosmic symbol of life, the conch had also the power to reveal any violation of the cosmic rhythms, or crime against society.

From Egyptian and Roman inscriptions, the scallop shell passed into Christian symbolism. By the Middle Ages, it was an emblem of the pilgrim, particularly to the shrine of St James of Compostela in Spain. Some explained that pilgrims used the shell as a drinking cup, or that is symbolised the sea shores of Compostela. But the purpose of a pilgrimage was still that of spiritual renewal, even though the true meaning of the shell had been forgotten.

ARROW

' How fleet is a glance of the mind!
Compared with the speed of its flight
The tempest itself lags behind,
And the swift-winged arrows of light '.
Verses Supposed to be Written by
Alexander Selkirk
William Cowper

THE ARROW IS a celestial weapon of the divine archer and sun god, Apollo. Forged for him by the lame blacksmith Hephaestus, Apollo's arrows are symbols of light and the rays of the sun, dispensing justice and death with their infallible aim. The ancient arrowhead was made of flint and shaped like a leaf, perhaps from a sacred tree of life. Descending from heaven, it was used as an amulet to preserve people and cattle from lightning. But when the American Indian feared that an eclipse was extinguishing his sun, he shot fire-tipped arrows back into the sky, to rekindle the heavenly light. For the Christians, an arrow also came to suggest a spiritual weapon, dedicated to the service of God, although it was an instrument of death for many of his martyrs. Because he would not renounce his faith, St Sebastian was pierced with arrows from the bows of Emperor Diocletian's guards. Strangely enough, the saint then became a protector of those threatened by the plague, since it was still believed that the dreaded disease was carried by the arrows of Apollo.

The sacred origin of the arrow made it an ancient instrument of divination called belomancy. It was practised among the Greeks and the Arabs, although the latter were forbidden to do so by the Koran. One method was to throw a number of arrows into the air and the direction in which the arrow inclined as it fell, pointed to the course to be taken. The *Book of Ezekiel* says: ' For the king of Babylon stood at the parting of the way, at the head of two ways, to use divination: he made his arrows bright, he consulted with images, he looked into the liver '.

ANCHOR

'Cast all your cares on God; that anchor holds'.
Enoch Arden
Alfred Lord Tennyson

THE ANCHOR, like the fish, first appeared carved in the catacombs of ancient Rome where the early Christian converts worshipped their new faith in secret. As a mystic symbol of hope, steadfastness and salvation it was often shown turned upside down, with a star, crescent or cross, and found engraved on gems and jewels of that period. Its meaning was derived from Paul's Epistle to the Hebrews in which he consoles those 'who have fled for refuge to lay hold upon the hope set before us: which hope we have as an anchor of the soul'.

St Nicholas of Myra, better known as Santa Clause, acquired the emblem of the anchor for calming the high seas on his voyage to the Holy Land. An anchor always beside him, his image is still to be found in almost every port throughout the world. In another Christian legend, St Clement of Rome, the possible successor to St Peter as Pope, was banished to the marble quarries of Crimea for refusing to deny his faith. There, his disciples suffered from the lack of water and he performed a miracle to quench their thirst. For this an anchor was tied around his neck and he was thrown into the sea by his oppressors. By the time of the Renaissance the emblem was widely known, and in art where every Christian virtue was personified, Hope always appeared as a winged woman with her hands raised to heaven and an anchor at her feet.

HORSESHOE

' For want of a nail the shoe is lost,
for want of a shoe the horse is lost,
for want of a horse the rider is lost '.
Jacula Prudentum
George Herbert

ALTHOUGH THE ancients protected the hoof of a horse with sandals and socks, the iron horseshoe was not introduced until the second century B.C., and was not commonly known or used until the Middle Ages. As a charm, its magic is partly inherited from the symbolism of the horse. In mythology and legend the animal has prophetic powers and is a friend of man. According to John Aubrey, the seventeenth century antiquarian, a horseshoe is a protection against witches. It is made of iron, the metal of Mars, and this planet is the foe of the god of witches, Saturn. Another theory is that the horseshoe repels evil because its womb-like shape is symbolic of goodness, fer-

tility and plenty. It is possible that the Romany gypsies, who wandered into every country in Europe, spread the belief in the protective powers and good luck of the horseshoe, as they introduced other beliefs and practices of sorcery and the black arts.

The power of a symbol lies not in the object itself but in the thought forces projected onto it, and these in time, make an object evil or good. There was even a horseshoe on the mast of Nelson's ship, the Victory. Nailed to doors, the two ends uppermost so that good fortune does not run out, the horseshoe is still the most popular lucky charm.